HOUGHTON MIFFLIN HARCOURT

Daily Language Workouts

Grade 4

Interactive Whiteboard Compatible!

Daily MUG Shot Sentences

Weekly MUG Shot Paragraphs

Writing Prompts

Writing Topics

Show-Me Sentences

GREAT SOURCE®

 HOUGHTON MIFFLIN HARCOURT

A Few Words About *Daily Language Workouts* Grade 4

Before you begin . . .

The activities in this book will help your students develop basic writing and language skills. You'll find three types of exercises on the following pages:

MUG Shot Sentences There are 175 sentences highlighting **m**echanics, **u**sage, and/or **g**rammar (MUG), one for each day of the school year. For the first 18 weeks, focused sentences concentrate on one skill per week. For the final 17 weeks, sentences present a mixed review, and students are asked to correct several types of errors in each sentence.

MUG Shot Paragraphs There are 35 weekly paragraphs. The first 18 correspond directly with each week's MUG Shot sentences, focusing on the same mechanics, usage, or grammar error. The final 17 paragraphs present a mixed review of the covered proofreading and editing skills.

Daily Writing Practice This section begins with **writing prompts** that include topics and graphics designed to inspire expository, narrative, descriptive, persuasive, and creative writing. Next, a discussion of daily journal writing introduces the lists of intriguing **writing topics.** Finally, the **show-me sentences** provide starting points for paragraphs, essays, and other writing forms.

Write Source Online provides the lessons in this book for interactive whiteboard instruction. To use, open the files from *Write Source Online* using your whiteboard software.

Photo Acknowledgements Cover ©VALUE STOCK IMAGES/age fotostock; 117 ©Digital Vision/Getty Images; 118, 136, 138 ©Corbis; 121 ©Ryan McVay/Lifesize/Getty Images; 123, 126, 135 ©Photodisc/Getty Images; 130 Harcourt School Publishers; 134 HMH Collection.

Printed in the U.S.A.

ISBN 978-0-547-48515-7

2 3 4 5 6 7 8 9 10 11 12 0956 15 14 13 12 11

4500295808 A B C D E F G

Table of Contents

Editing and Proofreading Marks

These symbols may be used to correct MUG Shot sentences and paragraphs.

Insert here.	∧	take ∧ home (them)
Insert a comma, a semicolon, or colon.	∧, ∧; ∧:	Troy, Michigan
Insert (add) a period.	⊙	Mrs⊙
Insert a hyphen.	∧ (-)	one-third cup
Insert a question mark or an exclamation point.	? ! ∧ ∧	How about you?
Capitalize a letter.	/ (or) ≡	T toronto (or) toronto ≡
Make a capital letter lowercase.	/	History (or) History (h)
Replace or delete (take out).	—— (or) ——℘	a ~~hot~~ day (cold) (or) a ~~hot~~ day
Insert an apostrophe or quotation marks.	∨' ∨" ∨"	Bill's "Wow!"
Use italics.	______	Tracker

MUG Shot Sentences

The MUG Shot sentences are designed to be used at the beginning of each class period as a quick and efficient way to review **m**echanics, **u**sage, and **g**rammar. Each sentence can be corrected and discussed in 3 to 5 minutes.

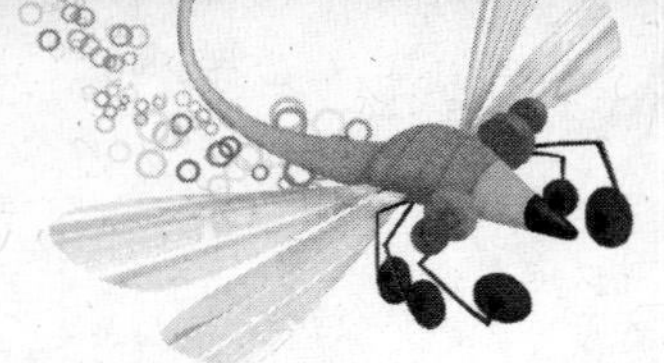

MUG Shot Sentence Organizer

Name ______________________ Date ______________

Corrected Sentence:

Corrected Sentence:

Corrected Sentence:

Corrected Sentence:

Corrected Sentence:

Implementation and Evaluation

The first 18 weeks of MUG Shot sentences are focused sentences. The sentences for each week usually focus on one proofreading skill. The remaining 17 weeks of MUG Shot sentences provide mixed reviews of two or three different proofreading skills per sentence.

Implementation

On the days that you use MUG Shot sentences, we suggest that you have students **correct the sentence orally.** After you write the sentence on the board, be sure to read it aloud to be sure students understand the sentence. Write the corrections on the board as a volunteer provides them. (The student may use the proofreading marks on page iv.) Have the student explain his or her corrections and discuss the results. If you wish, then ask all students to write the corrected form in their notebooks.

You may also **write a sentence on the board** at the beginning of the class period. Allow students time to read the sentence to themselves. (Make sure they understand the sentence.) Then have students correct each MUG Shot in a space reserved for them in their notebooks (or on a copy of the "MUG Shot Sentence Organizer" provided on page 2 of this book). Students may be supplied with a copy of the "Editing and Proofreading Marks" on page iv as a guide for marking changes to their MUG Shot sentences. Be sure to read each sentence aloud before students begin. Then have students in pairs or as a class discuss their corrections. Also make sure that each student understands why the corrections were made.

Each Friday, review the MUG Shots covered for the week. You might assign the MUG Shot paragraph that contains errors similar to the type students have worked on for the week. (See page 75.)

Evaluation

If you assign sentences daily, evaluate your students' work at the end of each week. We recommend that you give them a basic performance score for their work. This performance score might be based on having each sentence for that week written correctly in their language arts notebooks. You might also have students reflect on their MUG Shot work in a brief freewriting at the end of the week, or have them correct one or two review sentences. Consider asking the students to submit sentences for this review activity.

Note: In the MUG Shot sentences showing corrections for run-on sentences, sentence fragments, and sentence combining, one possible correction is shown. However, there are often a number of possible answers that would also be correct.

WEEK 1: The End of the Line

■ End Punctuation

Mirrors actually show reverse images of objects

■ End Punctuation

Did you know that California was named after a character in a popular Spanish novel

■ End Punctuation

Wake up, America—environmental awareness is back

■ End Punctuation

Tell me the name of the first English colony

■ End Punctuation

An African elephant could flap up a strong breeze with those ears, wouldn't you agree

WEEK 1: Corrected Sentences

■ End Punctuation

Mirrors actually show reverse images of objects.

■ End Punctuation

Did you know that California was named after a character in a popular Spanish novel?

■ End Punctuation

Wake up, America—environmental awareness is back! (or) .

■ End Punctuation

Tell me the name of the first English colony.

■ End Punctuation

An African elephant could flap up a strong breeze with those ears, wouldn't you agree?

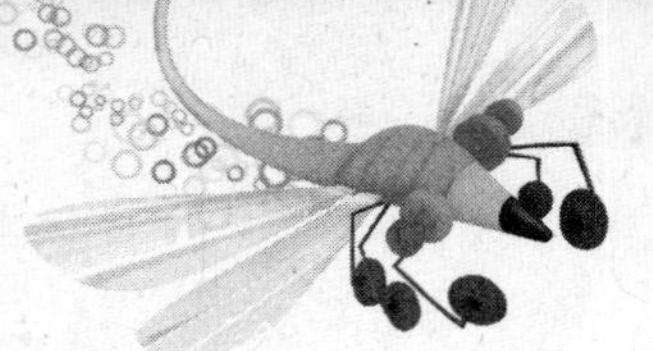

WEEK 2: *Get* in Line

■ Comma (Between Items in a Series)

The United States team at the first Olympics in 1896 consisted of seven runners a pole-vaulter a shot-putter and a hurdler.

■ Comma (Between Items in a Series)

On Saturday mornings, I watch cartoons eat breakfast help clean the house and wash the dog.

■ Comma (Between Items in a Series)

Here's a list of my least favorite vegetables: broccoli lima beans cauliflower beets and artichokes.

■ Comma (Between Items in a Series)

My favorite cars are high-powered sports cars hardtop convertibles and luxury-edition sport-utility vehicles.

■ Comma (Between Items in a Series)

Anteaters have eyes ears noses and mouths, but no teeth.

WEEK 2: Corrected Sentences

■ Comma (Between Items in a Series)

The United States team at the first Olympics in 1896 consisted of seven runners, a pole-vaulter, a shot-putter, and a hurdler.

■ Comma (Between Items in a Series)

On Saturday mornings, I watch cartoons, eat breakfast, help clean the house, and wash the dog.

■ Comma (Between Items in a Series)

Here's a list of my least favorite vegetables: broccoli, lima beans, cauliflower, beets, and artichokes.

■ Comma (Between Items in a Series)

My favorite cars are high-powered sports cars, hardtop convertibles, and luxury-edition sport-utility vehicles.

■ Comma (Between Items in a Series)

Anteaters have eyes, ears, noses, and mouths, but no teeth.

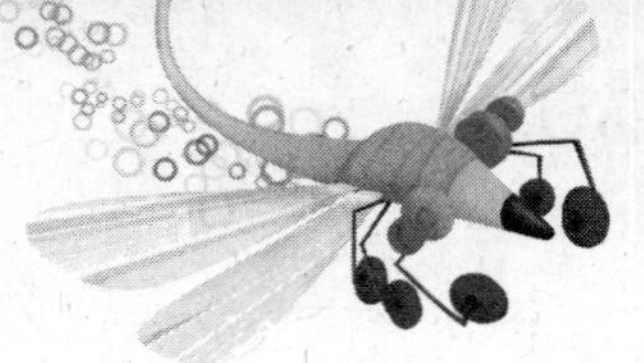

WEEK 3: Addressing the Issue

■ Comma (In Dates)

On June 16 1963 Valentina V. Tereshkova (a Russian) became the first woman to travel in outer space.

■ Comma (In Addresses)

Animal lovers may subscribe to *Ranger Rick* 11100 Wildlife Center Drive Reston Virginia 20190.

■ Comma (In Dates)

On July 4 1776 the American colonies declared their independence from Great Britain.

■ Comma (In Dates)

The English first celebrated May Day as a day to honor workers on May 1 1890.

■ Comma (In Dates and Addresses)

On June 25 2010 my family stayed in a motel at 5353 Midland Avenue Billings Montana.

WEEK 3: Corrected Sentences

Comma (In Dates)

On June 16, 1963, Valentina V. Tereshkova (a Russian) became the first woman to travel in outer space.

Comma (In Addresses)

Animal lovers may subscribe to *Ranger Rick*, 11100 Wildlife Center Drive, Reston, Virginia 20190.

Comma (In Dates)

On July 4, 1776, the American colonies declared their independence from Great Britain.

Comma (In Dates)

The English first celebrated May Day as a day to honor workers on May 1, 1890.

Comma (In Dates and Addresses)

On June 25, 2010, my family stayed in a motel at 5353 Midland Avenue, Billings, Montana.

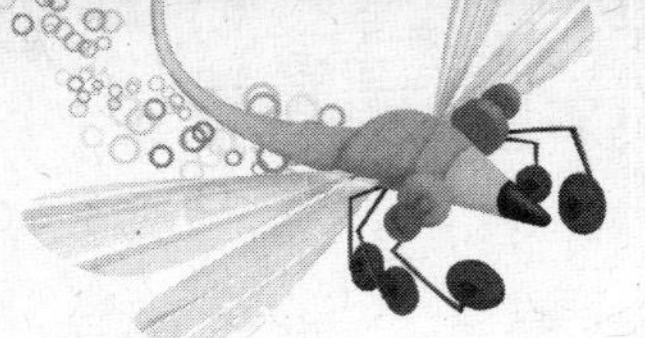

WEEK 4: A Number of Interruptions

■ Comma (To Keep Numbers Clear and To Set Off Interjections)

Hey if one centipede has 100 legs, do 100 centipedes have 100000 legs?

■ Comma (To Keep Numbers Clear)

A mile is just a mile unless it is 5280 feet, 1760 yards, or a little more than 1609 meters.

■ Comma (To Keep Numbers Clear)

The moon is only 2155 miles across, but the sun is 867000 miles across.

■ Comma (To Keep Numbers Clear)

Light travels at a speed of 186282 miles per second.

■ Comma (To Keep Numbers Clear and To Set Off Interjections)

A place in India once got 26466 millimeters of rain in a year. Wow that's 1042 inches!

WEEK 4: Corrected Sentences

■ Comma (To Keep Numbers Clear and To Set Off Interjections)

Hey, if one centipede has 100 legs, do 100 centipedes have 100,000 legs?

(Answer: No. They have 10,000 legs.)

■ Comma (To Keep Numbers Clear)

A mile is just a mile unless it is 5,280 feet, 1,760 yards, or a little more than 1,609 meters.

■ Comma (To Keep Numbers Clear)

The moon is only 2,155 miles across, but the sun is 867,000 miles across.

■ Comma (To Keep Numbers Clear)

Light travels at a speed of 186,282 miles per second.

■ Comma (To Keep Numbers Clear and To Set Off Interjections)

A place in India once got 26,466 millimeters of rain in a year. Wow, that's 1,042 inches!

WEEK 5: *Pause for a Clause*

■ Comma (In Compound Sentences)

I have never been to Alaska so I have never seen Mt. McKinley.

■ Comma (In Compound Sentences)

Most fish do not sleep but some types stand on their tails and lean against coral for a snooze.

■ Comma (In Compound Sentences)

After the first harvest, the Pilgrims held a feast for they wanted to show how thankful they were.

■ Comma (In Compound Sentences)

Andrew Jackson was born in South Carolina and he became the first man born in a log cabin to be elected president of the United States.

■ Comma (In Compound Sentences)

Quicksand can suck animals down to their deaths but a person can escape by lying flat and rolling out.

WEEK 5: Corrected Sentences

■ Comma (In Compound Sentences)

I have never been to Alaska, so I have never seen Mt. McKinley.

■ Comma (In Compound Sentences)

Most fish do not sleep, but some types stand on their tails and lean against coral for a snooze.

■ Comma (In Compound Sentences)

After the first harvest, the Pilgrims held a feast, for they wanted to show how thankful they were.

■ Comma (In Compound Sentences)

Andrew Jackson was born in South Carolina, and he became the first man born in a log cabin to be elected president of the United States.

■ Comma (In Compound Sentences)

Quicksand can suck animals down to their deaths, but a person can escape by lying flat and rolling out.

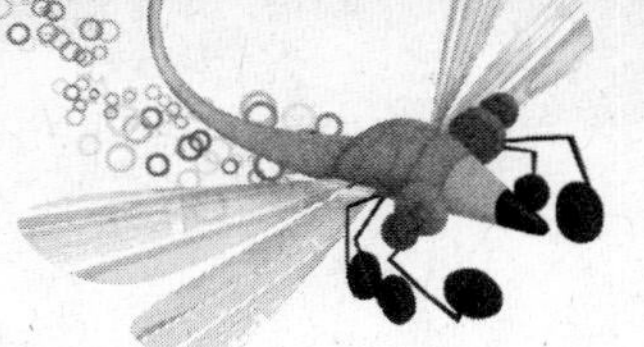

WEEK 6: Hyperlinks

■ Hyphen

Well informed football fans know that the Green Bay Packers beat the Kansas City Chiefs in the first Super Bowl.

■ Hyphen

My great aunt had 18 children; one half were boys, and the other half were girls.

■ Hyphen

The Beatles, a well known musical group, released 29 records in 1964.

■ Hyphen

The highest scoring basketball game ever occurred in 1983 when the Detroit Pistons outscored the Denver Nuggets, 186–184.

■ Hyphen

I would guess that two thirds of the class knows that you cannot divide a one syllable word at the end of a line.

WEEK 6: Corrected Sentences

■ Hyphen

Well-informed football fans know that the Green Bay Packers beat the Kansas City Chiefs in the first Super Bowl.

■ Hyphen

My great-aunt had 18 children; one-half were boys, and the other half were girls.

■ Hyphen

The Beatles, a well-known musical group, released 29 records in 1964.

■ Hyphen

The highest-scoring basketball game ever occurred in 1983 when the Detroit Pistons outscored the Denver Nuggets, 186–184.

■ Hyphen

I would guess that two-thirds of the class knows that you cannot divide a one-syllable word at the end of a line.

WEEK 7: It's All Yours

■ Apostrophe (In Contractions and To Form Possessives)

Although a flea isnt very big, the critters remarkable strength allows it to jump 200 times its length.

■ Apostrophe (To Form Possessives)

Koala bears main food is eucalyptus leaves.

■ Apostrophe (To Form Possessives)

Alexander Graham Bells first telephone was displayed in Philadelphias Exhibition Hall in 1876.

■ Apostrophe (To Form Possessives)

Harriet Beecher Stowes book *Uncle Toms Cabin* made people aware of the evils of slavery.

■ Apostrophe (To Form Possessives)

Charles Dickens books tell about his concern for the poor people of his day.

WEEK 7: Corrected Sentences

■ Apostrophe (In Contractions and To Form Possessives)

Although a flea isn't very big, the critter's remarkable strength allows it to jump 200 times its length.

■ Apostrophe (To Form Possessives)

Koala bears' main food is eucalyptus leaves.

■ Apostrophe (To Form Possessives)

Alexander Graham Bell's first telephone was displayed in Philadelphia's Exhibition Hall in 1876.

■ Apostrophe (To Form Possessives)

Harriet Beecher Stowe's book *Uncle Tom's Cabin* made people aware of the evils of slavery.

■ Apostrophe (To Form Possessives)

Charles ~~Dickens~~ Dickens' (or) Dickens's books tell about his concern for the poor people of his day.

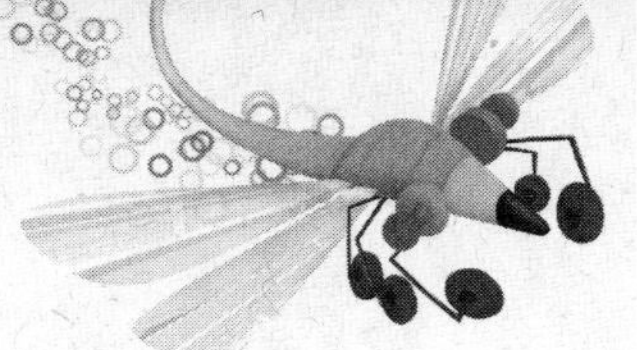

WEEK 8: And I Quote . . .

■ Quotation Marks

When astronaut Neil Armstrong stepped onto the moon, he said, That's one small step for a man, one giant leap for mankind.

■ Quotation Marks

The skydiving instructor asked, Who wants to go first?

■ Quotation Marks

Writer Sandra Cisneros says this about school: I didn't like school because all they saw was the outside of me.

■ Quotation Marks

Was it Eleanor Roosevelt who said, You must do the thing you think you cannot do?

■ Quotation Marks

I always laugh when I read Shel Silverstein's poem Jumping Rope.

WEEK 8: Corrected Sentences

■ Quotation Marks

When astronaut Neil Armstrong stepped onto the moon, he said, “That’s one small step for a man, one giant leap for mankind.”

■ Quotation Marks

The skydiving instructor asked, “Who wants to go first?”

■ Quotation Marks

Writer Sandra Cisneros says this about school: “I didn’t like school because all they saw was the outside of me.”

■ Quotation Marks

Was it Eleanor Roosevelt who said, “You must do the thing you think you cannot do”?

■ Quotation Marks

I always laugh when I read Shel Silverstein’s poem “Jumping Rope.”

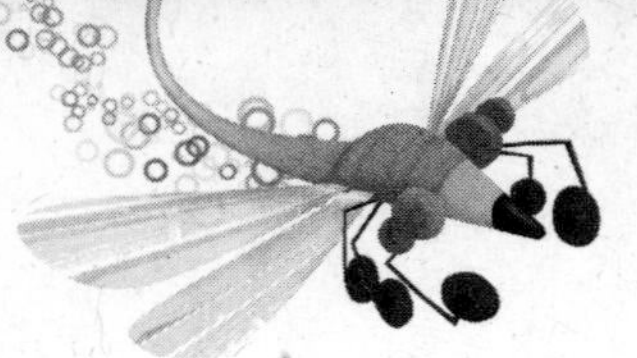

WEEK 9: *Capital Idea!*

■ Capitalization

the address for the Pro Football hall of fame is 2121 george halas drive, canton, ohio 44708.

■ Capitalization

elijah mcCoy's parents escaped from slavery in kentucky many years before the civil war.

■ Capitalization

today the people christopher columbus called indians are often called native americans.

■ Capitalization

my dad and I marched in the st. patrick's day parade in chicago.

■ Capitalization

jan e. matzeliger made the first shoe-stitching machine in the united states.

WEEK 9: Corrected Sentences

■ Capitalization

T H F G H D
the address for the Pro Football hall of fame is 2121 george halas drive,
C O
canton, ohio 44708.

■ Capitalization

E M K
elijah mcCoy's parents escaped from slavery in kentucky many years
C W
before the civil war.

■ Capitalization

T C C I
today the people christopher columbus called indians are often called
N A
native americans.

■ Capitalization

M S P D C
my dad and I marched in the st. patrick's day parade in chicago.

■ Capitalization

J E M U
jan e. matzeliger made the first shoe-stitching machine in the united
S
states.

WEEK 10: *Geographically Speaking*

■ Capitalization

The suez canal connects the mediterranean sea to the red sea.

■ Capitalization

many germans and scandinavians settled in the midwest.

■ Capitalization

The amazon river contains more water than the nile river, the mississippi river, and the yangtze river put together.

■ Capitalization

the empire state building in new york city is not as tall as the willis tower in chicago, illinois.

■ Capitalization

Would you rather visit redwood park in northern california or yosemite park in central california?

WEEK 10: Corrected Sentences

Capitalization

S C M S R S
The suez canal connects the mediterranean sea to the red sea.

Capitalization

M G S M
many germans and scandinavians settled in the midwest.

Capitalization

A R N R M
The amazon river contains more water than the nile river, the mississippi
R Y R
river, and the yangtze river put together.

Capitalization

T E S B N Y C W
the empire state building in new york city is not as tall as the willis
T C I
tower in chicago, illinois.

Capitalization

R P C Y
Would you rather visit redwood park in northern california or yosemite
P C
park in central california?

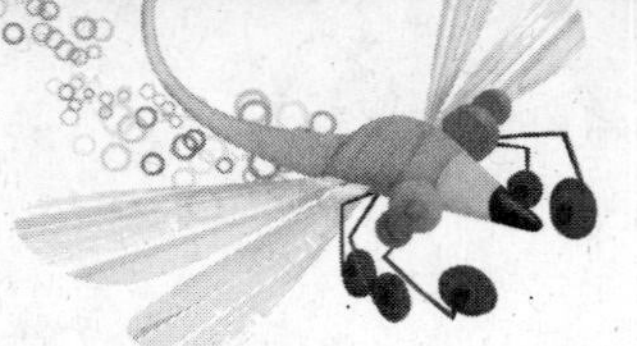

WEEK 11: *One Is a Lonely Number*

■ Plurals

We grabbed our paintes and brushs and headed for the art room.

■ Plurals

My mother uses her sharpest knifes to cut the loafs of bread.

■ Plurals

Pianoes are popular because they can produce a wide range of soundes.

■ Plurals

My little brother enjoys chasing bunnys and gooses at the park.

■ Plurals

For supper, Mom prepared two platesful of tacoes and burritos.

WEEK 11: Corrected Sentences

■ Plurals

We grabbed our ~~paintes~~ paints and ~~brushs~~ brushes and headed for the art room.

■ Plurals

My mother uses her sharpest ~~knifes~~ knives to cut the ~~loafs~~ loaves of bread.

■ Plurals

~~Pianoes~~ Pianos are popular because they can produce a wide range of ~~soundes~~ sounds.

■ Plurals

My little brother enjoys chasing ~~bunnys~~ bunnies and ~~gooses~~ geese at the park.

■ Plurals

For supper, Mom prepared two ~~platesful~~ platefuls of ~~tacoes~~ tacos and burritos.

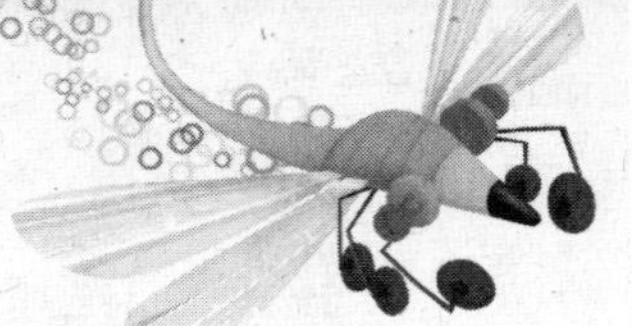

WEEK 12: One Potato, Two Potato, Three Potato, Four

■ Numbers

The Pacific Ocean covers 64,000,000 square miles.

■ Numbers

Native Americans make up less than one percent of the United States population; more than nine-hundred thousand Native Americans live in Oklahoma, California, and Arizona.

■ Numbers

In the year two thousand and seven, the population of the United States was more than three hundred million.

■ Numbers

About one out of every 5 people in the world is Chinese.

■ Numbers

36,000,000 people live in California, while only five-hundred thousand people live in Wyoming.

WEEK 12: Corrected Sentences

■ Numbers

64 million
The Pacific Ocean covers ~~64,000,000~~ square miles.

■ Numbers

1
Native Americans make up less than ~~one~~ percent of the United States

900,000
population; more than ~~nine-hundred thousand~~ Native Americans live in Oklahoma, California, and Arizona.

■ Numbers

2007
In the year ~~two thousand and seven~~, the population of the United States

300
was more than ~~three hundred~~ million.

■ Numbers

1
About ~~one~~ out of every 5 people in the world is Chinese.

■ Numbers

Thirty-six million 500,000
~~36,000,000~~ people live in California, while only ~~five-hundred thousand~~ people live in Wyoming.

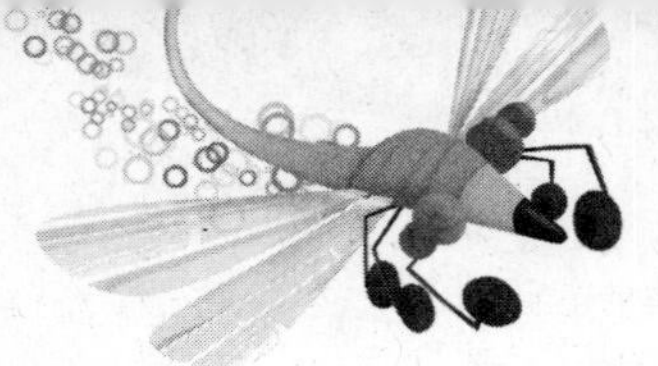

WEEK 13: *Reaching an Agreement*

■ Subject-Verb Agreement

Cirrus clouds is the highest clouds in the sky.

■ Subject-Verb Agreement

Winter winds usually blows from north to south.

■ Subject-Verb Agreement

Sedimentary rocks is made of pieces of various types of rocks, minerals, plants, or organisms.

■ Subject-Verb Agreement

Nobody know who invented eyeglasses, but they is very useful.

■ Subject-Verb Agreement

The air in tornadoes spin in a circle.

WEEK 13: Corrected Sentences

■ Subject-Verb Agreement

Cirrus clouds ~~is~~ *are* the highest clouds in the sky.

■ Subject-Verb Agreement

Winter winds usually ~~blows~~ *blow* from north to south.

■ Subject-Verb Agreement

Sedimentary rocks ~~is~~ *are* made of pieces of various types of rocks, minerals, plants, or organisms.

■ Subject-Verb Agreement

Nobody ~~know~~ *knows* who invented eyeglasses, but they ~~is~~ *are* very useful.

■ Subject-Verb Agreement

The air in tornadoes ~~spin~~ *spins* in a circle.

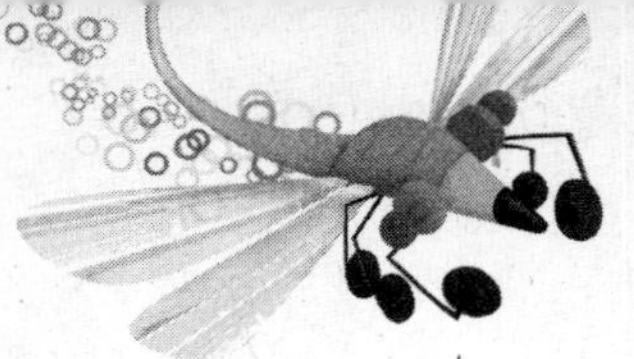

WEEK 14: *Yes, I Agree*

■ Subject-Verb Agreement

Eagles, pelicans, and trumpeter swans has been seen in Yellowstone National Park.

■ Subject-Verb Agreement

New York, New Jersey, and Pennsylvania is called the Middle Atlantic States.

■ Subject-Verb Agreement

Was Christopher Columbus and Vasco da Gama great explorers?

■ Subject-Verb Agreement

My grandparents always comes to my soccer games.

■ Subject-Verb Agreement

There are a dogsled race each year in Alaska from Anchorage to Nome.

WEEK 14: Corrected Sentences

■ Subject-Verb Agreement

Eagles, pelicans, and trumpeter swans ~~has~~ *have* been seen in Yellowstone National Park.

■ Subject-Verb Agreement

New York, New Jersey, and Pennsylvania ~~is~~ *are* called the Middle Atlantic States.

■ Subject-Verb Agreement

~~Was~~ *Were* Christopher Columbus and Vasco da Gama great explorers?

■ Subject-Verb Agreement

My grandparents always ~~comes~~ *come* to my soccer games.

■ Subject-Verb Agreement

There ~~are~~ *is* a dogsled race each year in Alaska from Anchorage to Nome.

WEEK 15: Runaway Sentences

■ Run-On Sentence

Pocahontas saved the life of John Smith she later married another settler.

■ Run-On Sentence

A triathlon is a three-part race it includes swimming, running, and biking.

■ Run-On Sentence

Russia is the largest country in the world Canada is the second largest.

■ Run-On Sentence

On September 6, 1995, Cal Ripken broke one of baseball's most amazing records he played his 2,131st straight game.

■ Run-On Sentence

What is the Liberty Bell why is it important?

WEEK 15: Corrected Sentences (Answers may vary.)

■ Run-On Sentence

Pocahontas saved the life of John Smith, but she later married another settler.

■ Run-On Sentence

A triathlon is a three-part race. It includes swimming, running, and biking.

■ Run-On Sentence

Russia is the largest country in the world. Canada is the second largest.

■ Run-On Sentence

On September 6, 1995, Cal Ripken broke one of baseball's most amazing records. He played his 2,131st straight game.

■ Run-On Sentence

What is the Liberty Bell? Why is it important?

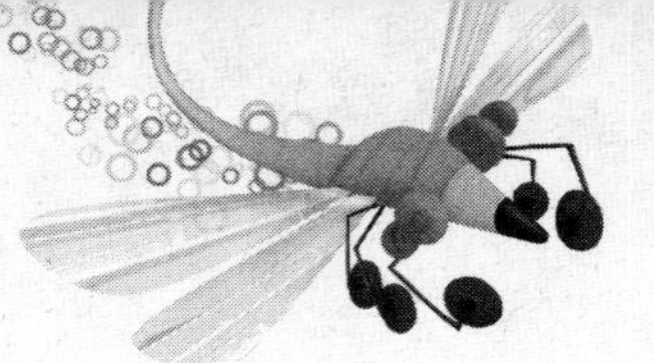

WEEK 16: Bits and Pieces

■ Sentence Fragment

An example of a kind person.

■ Sentence Fragment

Nervously waited for my friend to show up.

■ Sentence Fragment

Down the driveway, across the yard, over the fence, and through the alley.

■ Sentence Fragment

The person in my family with the best sense of humor.

■ Sentence Fragment

Gathered up my books by my locker.

WEEK 16: Corrected Sentences (Answers will vary.)

■ Sentence Fragment

Mr. Gardner is
An example of a kind person.

■ Sentence Fragment

I
Nervously waited for my friend to show up.

■ Sentence Fragment

The dog chased my cat
Down the driveway, across the yard, over the fence, and through the alley.

■ Sentence Fragment

is my sister Hillary.
The person in my family with the best sense of humor.

■ Sentence Fragment

After school, I
Gathered up my books by my locker.

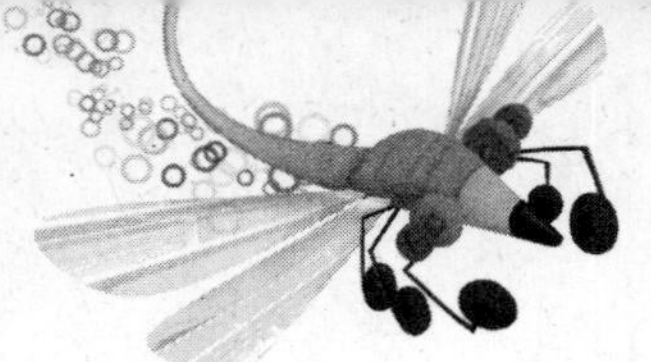

WEEK 17: The Right Way

■ Using the Right Word

Their is no real reason why painters where white, but that's the weigh they dress.

■ Using the Right Word

Dogs tilt there heads to the side too here you're voice.

■ Using the Right Word

Principles are people with strong principals.

■ Using the Right Word

Hour science teacher is going two learn us about the whole in the ozone layer.

■ Using the Right Word

Sum stationary seams too pretty too right on.

WEEK 17: Corrected Sentences

■ Using the Right Word

There wear way
~~Their~~ is no real reason why painters ~~where~~ white, but that's the ~~weigh~~ they dress.

■ Using the Right Word

their to hear your
Dogs tilt ~~there~~ heads to the side ~~too~~ ~~here~~ ~~you're~~ voice.

■ Using the Right Word

Principals principles
~~Principles~~ are people with strong ~~principals~~.

■ Using the Right Word

Our to teach hole
~~Hour~~ science teacher is going ~~two~~ ~~learn~~ us about the ~~whole~~ in the ozone layer.

■ Using the Right Word

Some stationery seems to write
~~Sum~~ ~~stationary~~ ~~seams~~ too pretty ~~too~~ ~~right~~ on.

WEEK 18: A Combination of Factors

■ Compound Sentences

Math was very hard yesterday and today. I'm going to ask for special help.

■ Combine Sentences with Key Words and Phrases

Earth orbits our sun. Eight other planets orbit our sun.

■ Compound Sentences

Everyone likes cute, furry animals. Naturalists even like spiders and insects.

■ Combine Sentences with Key Words and Phrases

One American mile equals 5,280 feet. One American mile equals 1,609.3 meters.

■ Combine Sentences with Key Words and Phrases

Lobsters have large claws. Lobsters run backward. Lobsters taste good when cooked and buttered.

WEEK 18: Corrected Sentences (Answers will vary.)

Compound Sentences

Math was very hard yesterday and today, so I'm going to ask for special help.

Combine Sentences with Key Words and Phrases

Earth ~~orbits our sun~~ and eight other planets orbit our sun.

Compound Sentences

Everyone likes cute, furry animals, but naturalists even like spiders and insects.

Combine Sentences with Key Words and Phrases

One American mile equals 5,280 feet ~~One American mile equals~~ or 1,609.3 meters.

Combine Sentences with Key Words and Phrases

Lobsters have large claws, ~~Lobsters~~ run backward, and ~~Lobsters~~ taste good when cooked and buttered.

WEEK 19: History of Language

■ Using the Right Word, Capitalization, Numbers

Their are twenty-six letters in the english alphabet.

■ Comma (To Separate Introductory Phrases and Clauses), Verb (Irregular), Pronoun-Antecedent Agreement

At one time in its history the Greeks writed from right to left.

■ Capitalization, Improving Spelling

I beleive the semites were the first people to use pictures as words.

■ Capitalization, Comma (To Set Off Appositives)

The egyptians invented hieroglyphics a kind of picture writing 5,000 years ago.

■ Capitalization, Subject-Verb Agreement, Run-On Sentence

Today, deaf people uses Sign language they use it to talk to other people.

WEEK 19: Corrected Sentences

■ Using the Right Word, Capitalization, Numbers

There 26 E

~~Their~~ are ~~twenty-six~~ letters in the english alphabet.

■ Comma (To Separate Introductory Phrases and Clauses), Verb (Irregular), Pronoun-Antecedent Agreement

their wrote

At one time in ~~its~~ history, the Greeks ~~writed~~ from right to left.

■ Capitalization, Improving Spelling

believe S

I ~~beleive~~ the semites were the first people to use pictures as words.

■ Capitalization, Comma (To Set Off Appositives)

E

The egyptians invented hieroglyphics, a kind of picture writing, 5,000 years ago.

■ Capitalization, Subject-Verb Agreement, Run-On Sentence

use T

Today, deaf people ~~uses~~ Sign language. they use it to talk to other people.

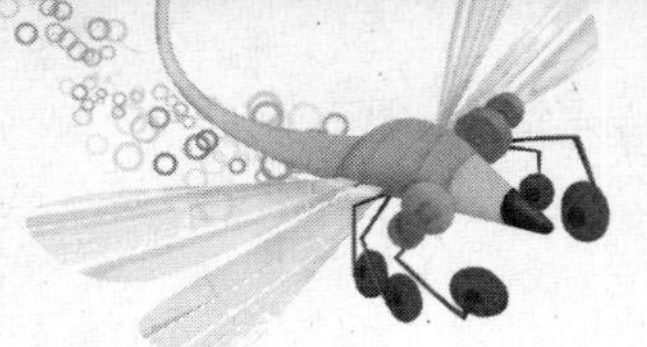

WEEK 20: The English Language

■ Verb (Irregular), Capitalization, Comma (Between Items in a Series)

English was spoke only by people in the British Isles until the british empire spread the language to america africa australia and the Far East.

■ Comma (To Separate Introductory Phrases and Clauses), Pronoun-Antecedent Agreement

Because English is spoken throughout the world they is being called the first global language.

■ Numbers, Subject-Verb Agreement

The English language have more words (close to 1,000,000) than the German language (only one hundred and eighty-five thousand).

■ Apostrophe (To Form Possessives), Numbers, Adjective (Comparative/Superlative)

Of all the worlds two thousand and seven hundred languages, English has the most richest vocabulary.

■ Hyphen, Comma (In Direct Address), Verb (Irregular)

Diane did you know three fourths of the world's mail today is writed in English?

WEEK 20: Corrected Sentences

■ Verb (Irregular), Capitalization, Comma (Between Items in a Series)

English was ~~spoke~~ spoken only by people in the British Isles until the ~~british~~ British ~~empire~~ Empire spread the language to ~~america~~ America, ~~africa~~ Africa, ~~australia~~ Australia, and the Far East.

■ Comma (To Separate Introductory Phrases and Clauses), Pronoun-Antecedent Agreement

Because English is spoken throughout the world, ~~they~~ it is being called the first global language.

■ Numbers, Subject-Verb Agreement

The English language ~~have~~ has more words (close to ~~1,000,000~~ 1 million) than the German language (only ~~one hundred and eighty five thousand~~ 185,000).

■ Apostrophe (To Form Possessives), Numbers, Adjective (Comparative/Superlative)

Of all the world's ~~two thousand and seven hundred~~ 2,700 languages, English has the ~~most~~ richest vocabulary.

■ Hyphen, Comma (In Direct Address), Verb (Irregular)

Diane, did you know three-fourths of the world's mail today is ~~writed~~ written in English?

WEEK 21: *Something Fishy*

■ **Comma (To Set Off Interjections), Numbers, Using the Right Word**

Wow a female herring lies 30 thousand eggs at once!

■ **Pronoun-Antecedent Agreement, Apostrophe (To Form Possessives), Comma (In Direct Address)**

Shelly did you know that the male sea horse protects the mothers eggs by keeping it in a pouch on his stomach?

■ **Using the Right Word, Semicolon, Adjective (Comparative/Superlative)**

One of the most unusualest fish is the flounder both eyes are on one side of it's body.

■ **Plurals, Semicolon**

The archerfish knocks insects off leafs it shoots a stream of water at them.

■ **Comma (In Compound Sentences and To Separate Equal Adjectives), Pronoun-Antecedent Agreement**

Tropical fish must live in clear warm water or it will die.

WEEK 21: Corrected Sentences

■ Comma (To Set Off Interjections), Numbers, Using the Right Word

Wow, a female herring ~~lies~~ lays ~~30 thousand~~ 30,000 eggs at once!

■ Pronoun-Antecedent Agreement, Apostrophe (To Form Possessives), Comma (In Direct Address)

Shelly, did you know that the male sea horse protects the mother's eggs by keeping ~~it~~ them in a pouch on his stomach?

■ Using the Right Word, Semicolon, Adjective (Comparative/Superlative)

One of the most ~~unusualest~~ unusual fish is the flounder; both eyes are on one side of ~~it's~~ its body.

■ Plurals, Semicolon

The archerfish knocks insects off ~~leafs~~ leaves; it shoots a stream of water at them.

■ Comma (In Compound Sentences and To Separate Equal Adjectives), Pronoun-Antecedent Agreement

Tropical fish must live in clear, warm water, or ~~it~~ they will die.

WEEK 22: Animals on Parade

■ Plurals, Using the Right Word, Rambling Sentence

Kangarooes are amazing animals who live in Australia and can really jump and large ones can cover more then 30 feet with one leap!

■ Adjective (Comparative/Superlative), Capitalization, Hyphen

My five year old golden Retriever is the most calm dog in all of dade county.

■ Using the Right Word, Improving Spelling

Female black widow spiders have poisenous bites and sometimes kill there mates.

■ Using the Right Word, Subject-Verb Agreement

A few animals sea in color, but most animals sees only shades of gray.

■ Colon, Using the Right Word, Comma (Between Items in a Series)

Movies have been maid from the following books *Babe: The Gallant Pig* *Stuart Little* *The Iron Giant* and *The Borrowers.*

WEEK 22: Corrected Sentences

■ Plurals, Using the Right Word, Rambling Sentence

~~Kangarooes~~ Kangaroos are amazing animals ~~who~~ that live in Australia. ~~and~~ They can really jump, and large ones can cover more ~~then~~ than 30 feet with one leap!

■ Adjective (Comparative/Superlative), Capitalization, Hyphen

My five-year-old golden ~~Retriever~~ retriever is the ~~most calm~~ calmest dog in all of ~~dade~~ Dade ~~county~~ County.

■ Using the Right Word, Improving Spelling

Female black widow spiders have ~~poisenous~~ poisonous bites and sometimes kill ~~there~~ their mates.

■ Using the Right Word, Subject-Verb Agreement

A few animals ~~sea~~ see in color, but most animals ~~sees~~ see only shades of gray.

■ Colon, Using the Right Word, Comma (Between Items in a Series)

Movies have been ~~maid~~ made from the following books: *Babe: The Gallant Pig*, *Stuart Little*, *The Iron Giant*, and *The Borrowers.*

WEEK 23: Maps, Maps, Maps

■ Capitalization, Comma (Between Items in a Series and To Set Off Appositives)

The Gulf Stream a warm ocean current flows from the gulf of mexico past the east coast of Florida to the North Atlantic Ocean.

■ Comma (In Direct Address), Subject-Verb Agreement, Plurals

John seas is large bodys of salt water partly surrounded by land.

■ Quotation Marks, Comma (To Set Off Dialogue), Period

Mr Baily said Look up the Galápagos Islands on your maps and write down their latitude and longitude.

■ Capitalization, Run-On Sentence, Improving Spelling

In 1849, a great flood of setlers headed west they followed a map of oregon and california made in 1848.

■ Comma (To Separate Introductory Phrases and Clauses), Improving Spelling, Apostrophe (In Contractions)

If you find the Great Lakes on a map youll see four of them share thier borders with Canada and the United States.

WEEK 23: Corrected Sentences

■ Capitalization, Comma (Between Items in a Series and To Set Off Appositives)

The Gulf Stream a warm ocean current flows from the gulf of mexico past the east coast of Florida to the North Atlantic Ocean.

■ Comma (In Direct Address), Subject-Verb Agreement, Plurals

John seas is large bodys of salt water partly surrounded by land.

■ Quotation Marks, Comma (To Set Off Dialogue), Period

Mr Baily said Look up the Galápagos Islands on your maps and write down their latitude and longitude.

■ Capitalization, Run-On Sentence, Improving Spelling

In 1849, a great flood of setlers headed west they followed a map of oregon and california made in 1848.

■ Comma (To Separate Introductory Phrases and Clauses), Improving Spelling, Apostrophe (In Contractions)

If you find the Great Lakes on a map youll see four of them share thier borders with Canada and the United States.

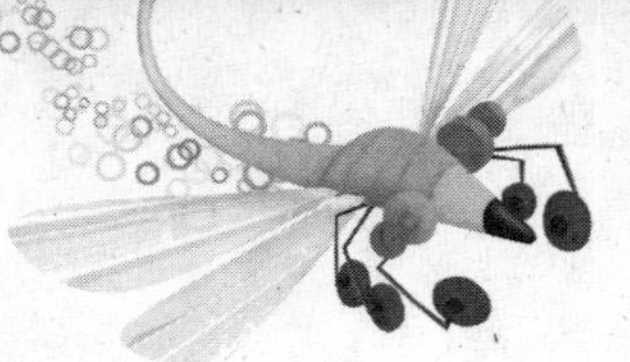

WEEK 24: *On a Map . . .*

■ Using the Right Word, Comma (To Keep Numbers Clear), Capitalization

They're more than 7100 islands that make up the country called the philippines.

■ Using the Right Word, Capitalization, Semicolon

The equator goes from East to West it passes threw South America and Africa.

■ Italics and Underlining, Sentence Fragment, Comma (In Direct Address)

Did you know that the Caspian Sea is actually a lake Tom? The world's largest saltwater lake (the word sea means a great body of salty water).

■ Capitalization, Run-On Sentence, Apostrophe (To Form Possessives)

Minnesota has the largest scandinavian population in the United States Duluth, on the shores of lake superior, is the countrys largest inland port.

■ Comma (To Separate Introductory Phrases and Clauses), Capitalization, Using the Right Word

Before reading this sentence did you know that the capitol of Canada is ottawa?

WEEK 24: Corrected Sentences

Using the Right Word, Comma (To Keep Numbers Clear), Capitalization

There are
~~They're~~ more than 7,100 islands that make up the country called the
P
philippines.

Using the Right Word, Capitalization, Semicolon

e w through
The equator goes from East to West; it passes ~~threw~~ South America and Africa.

Italics and Underlining, Sentence Fragment, Comma (In Direct Address)

It's t
Did you know that the Caspian Sea is actually a lake, Tom? The world's largest saltwater lake (the word sea means a great body of salty water).

Capitalization, Run-On Sentence, Apostrophe (To Form Possessives)

S
Minnesota has the largest scandinavian population in the United States.
L S '
Duluth, on the shores of lake superior, is the country's largest inland port.

Comma (To Separate Introductory Phrases and Clauses), Capitalization, Using the Right Word

capital
Before reading this sentence, did you know that the ~~capitol~~ of Canada is
O
ottawa?

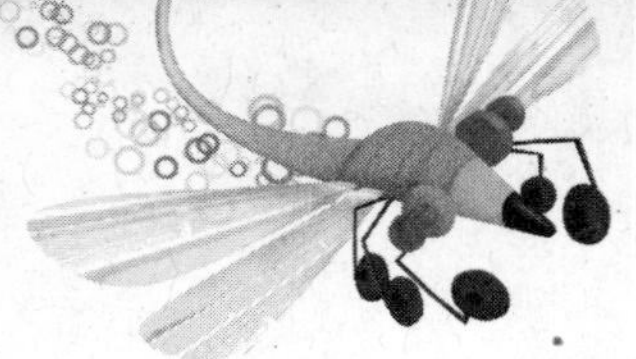

WEEK 25: *Where in the World?*

■ Sentence Fragment, Numbers

Canada a large country with a small population of 27,000,000 people.

■ Comma (To Keep Numbers Clear and To Separate Equal Adjectives), Apostrophe (To Form Possessives)

Chinas first emperor was buried with an army of 7500 life-sized clay soldiers.

■ Using the Right Word, Semicolon, Adjective (Comparative/Superlative)

The Sahara Dessert may be the most hottest place on earth it holds the record temperature of 136.4 degrees Fahrenheit.

■ Using the Right Word, Comma (To Set Off Appositives)

The Czech Republic and Slovakia two of the newest nations in the world used too be called Czechoslovakia.

■ Comma (To Separate Introductory Phrases and Clauses), Capitalization, Subject-Verb Agreement

When you is at the north pole the only direction you can go is South.

WEEK 25: Corrected Sentences

■ Sentence Fragment, Numbers

Canada is a large country with a small population of ~~27,000,000~~ 27 million people.

■ Comma (To Keep Numbers Clear and To Separate Equal Adjectives), Apostrophe (To Form Possessives)

China's first emperor was buried with an army of 7,500 life-sized, clay soldiers.

■ Using the Right Word, Semicolon, Adjective (Comparative/Superlative)

The Sahara ~~Dessert~~ Desert may be the ~~most~~ hottest place on earth; it holds the record temperature of 136.4 degrees Fahrenheit.

■ Using the Right Word, Comma (To Set Off Appositives)

The Czech Republic and Slovakia, two of the newest nations in the world, used ~~too~~ to be called Czechoslovakia.

■ Comma (To Separate Introductory Phrases and Clauses), Capitalization, Subject-Verb Agreement

When you ~~is~~ are at the North Pole, the only direction you can go is south.

WEEK 26: *Colors and Symbols*

■ Comma (To Separate Introductory Phrases and Clauses), Using the Right Word, Apostrophe (In Contractions)

If you lived in ancient Rome you couldnt where purple unless you were a member of the emperor's family.

■ Comma (To Set Off Appositives), Capitalization, Using the Right Word

At won time in French history, only the Princess could wear scarlet a bright read color.

■ Using the Right Word, Plurals

Because they're were no sidewalkes long ago, people would roll out a red carpet for the royal family's too walk on.

■ Plurals, Numbers, Sentence Fragment

Wonder why most countrys have 3 colores in their flags.

■ Quotation Marks, Double Negatives, Comma (To Set Off Dialogue)

Yesterday our teacher told us Class, some people say that Betsy Ross didn't never design the American flag; some say Francis Hopkinson did that.

WEEK 26: Corrected Sentences

■ Comma (To Separate Introductory Phrases and Clauses), Using the Right Word, Apostrophe (In Contractions)

If you lived in ancient Rome, you couldn't ~~where~~ wear purple unless you were a member of the emperor's family.

■ Comma (To Set Off Appositives), Capitalization, Using the Right Word

At ~~won~~ one time in French history, only the ~~Princess~~ princess could wear scarlet, a bright ~~read~~ red color.

■ Using the Right Word, Plurals

Because ~~they're~~ there were no ~~sidewalkes~~ sidewalks long ago, people would roll out a red carpet for the royal ~~family's~~ families ~~too~~ to walk on.

■ Plurals, Numbers, Sentence Fragment

I ~~Wonder~~ wonder why most ~~countrys~~ countries have ~~3 colores~~ three colors in their flags.

■ Quotation Marks, Double Negatives, Comma (To Set Off Dialogue)

Yesterday our teacher told us, "Class, some people say that Betsy Ross didn't ~~never~~ design the American flag; some say Francis Hopkinson did that."

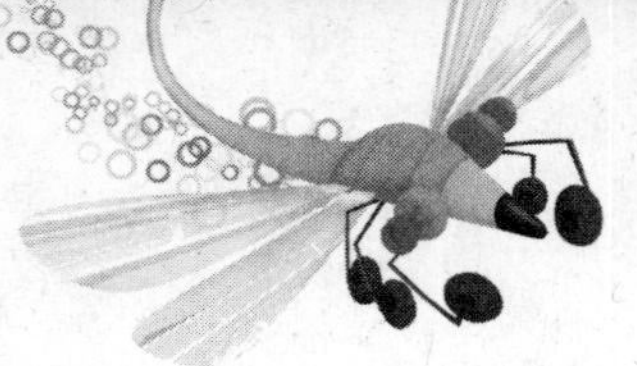

WEEK 27: Signs and Symbols

■ Comma (In Compound Sentences), Subject-Verb Agreement, End Punctuation

School-crossing signs are yellow but what color is hospital signs.

■ Using the Right Word, Comma (Between Items in a Series), Verb (Irregular)

I want my little brother two be safe on his bike, sew I teached him that red means stop yellow means caution and green means go.

■ Comma (To Separate Introductory Phrases and Clauses), Hyphen, Using the Right Word

When people go walking at night they should where reflective material or light colored clothing.

■ Subject-Verb Agreement, Comma (To Separate Equal Adjectives)

To help keep them safe on the job, construction workers wears brightly colored hard hats and heavy metal-toed boots.

■ Subject-Verb Agreement, Using the Right Word

Wires used buy electricians is color coded to prevent accidents and fires.

WEEK 27: Corrected Sentences

■ Comma (In Compound Sentences), Subject-Verb Agreement, End Punctuation

School-crossing signs are yellow, but what color ~~is~~ are hospital signs~~.~~?

■ Using the Right Word, Comma (Between Items in a Series), Verb (Irregular)

I want my little brother ~~two~~ to be safe on his bike, ~~sew~~ so I ~~teached~~ taught him that red means stop, yellow means caution, and green means go.

■ Comma (To Separate Introductory Phrases and Clauses), Hyphen, Using the Right Word

When people go walking at night, they should ~~where~~ wear reflective material or light-colored clothing.

■ Subject-Verb Agreement, Comma (To Separate Equal Adjectives)

To help keep them safe on the job, construction workers ~~wears~~ wear brightly colored hard hats and heavy, metal-toed boots.

■ Subject-Verb Agreement, Using the Right Word

Wires used ~~buy~~ by electricians ~~is~~ are color coded to prevent accidents and fires.

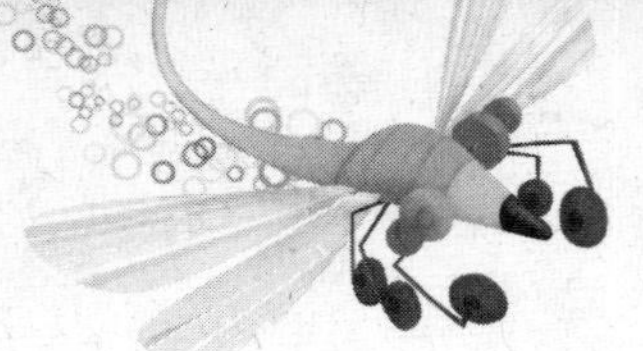

WEEK 28: U.S. History

■ Using the Right Word, Italics and Underlining, Capitalization

Thomas Paine helped americans understand the true meaning of freedom by righting The Age of Reason and other books.

■ Abbreviations, Numbers, Period

In nineteen ninety, L Douglas Wilder became the first African American elected governor in the U.S.

■ Comma (To Separate Introductory Phrases and Clauses), Capitalization, Using the Right Word

Though you probably no the first president of the united states do you know the first vice president?

■ Run-On Sentence, Verb (Irregular), Comma (To Keep Numbers Clear), Quotation Marks

My history teacher said, The first American train robbery taked place in 1866 the robbers made off with $16000.

■ Comma (To Set Off Appositives), Capitalization, Verb (Irregular)

George Washington the first president of the united States was sweared into office in New York City.

WEEK 28: Corrected Sentences

■ Using the Right Word, Italics and Underlining, Capitalization

Thomas Paine helped ~~a~~ A mericans understand the true meaning of freedom by ~~righting~~ writing <u>The Age of Reason</u> and other books.

■ Abbreviations, Numbers, Period

In ~~nineteen ninety,~~ 1990, L[.] Douglas Wilder became the first African American elected governor in the ~~U.S.~~ United States.

■ Comma (To Separate Introductory Phrases and Clauses), Capitalization, Using the Right Word

Though you probably ~~no~~ know the first president of the ~~u~~ U nited ~~s~~ S tates[,] do you know the first vice president?

■ Run-On Sentence, Verb (Irregular), Comma (To Keep Numbers Clear), Quotation Marks

My history teacher said, [“]The first American train robbery ~~taked~~ took place in 1866[;] the robbers made off with $16[,]000.[”]

■ Comma (To Set Off Appositives), Capitalization, Verb (Irregular)

George Washington[,] the first president of the ~~u~~ U nited States[,] was ~~sweared~~ sworn into office in New York City.

WEEK 29: The Civil War and Before

■ Using the Right Word, Numbers

Native Americans lived hear for thousands of years before Columbus "discovered" America in fourteen ninety-two.

■ Numbers, Comma (In Addresses), Run-On Sentence

The first Spanish colony in America was established in Pensacola Florida in 1559 it lasted only 2 years.

■ Comma (In Compound Sentences), Using the Right Word, Capitalization

The South eventually decided to brake away from the Union and the southern states formed the confederate states of america.

■ Run-On Sentence, Verb (Irregular)

General Robert E. Lee leaded the army for the South Ulysses S. Grant becomed the top general for the North.

■ Capitalization, Comma (In Addresses), Abbreviations

The confederate states of America established their capital in richmond VA.

WEEK 29: Corrected Sentences

■ Using the Right Word, Numbers

Native Americans lived ~~hear~~ [here] for thousands of years before Columbus "discovered" America in ~~fourteen ninety-two~~ [1492].

■ Numbers, Comma (In Addresses), Run-On Sentence

The first Spanish colony in America was established in Pensacola[,] Florida[,] in 1559. ~~it~~ [I]t lasted only ~~2~~ [two] years.

■ Comma (In Compound Sentences), Using the Right Word, Capitalization

The South eventually decided to ~~brake~~ [break] away from the Union[,] and the southern states formed the ~~c~~[C]onfederate ~~s~~[S]tates of ~~a~~[A]merica.

■ Run-On Sentence, Verb (Irregular)

General Robert E. Lee ~~leaded~~ [led] the army for the South. Ulysses S. Grant ~~becomed~~ [became] the top general for the North.

■ Capitalization, Comma (In Addresses), Abbreviations

The ~~c~~[C]onfederate ~~s~~[S]tates of America established their capital in ~~r~~[R]ichmond[,] ~~VA~~ [Virginia].

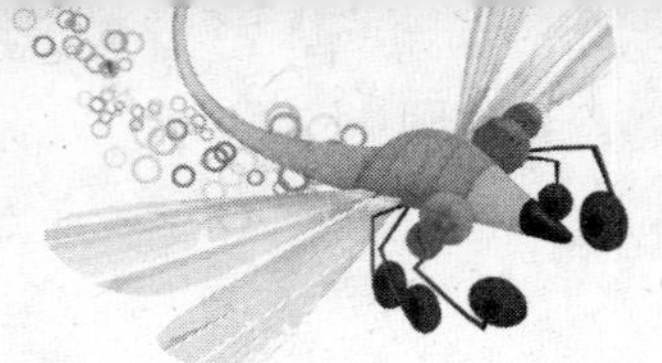

WEEK 30: *Science* Now and Then

■ Colon, Numbers, Quotation Marks (For Special Words)

Our science class met at 1030 this morning in the park, and Mr. Bartz showed us the fifty annual rings on a cross section of a freshly cut tree.

■ Capitalization, Comma (To Separate Introductory Phrases and Clauses)

After five walks in space astronauts were able to repair the hubble telescope.

■ Subject-Verb Agreement, Adjective (Comparative/Superlative), Using the Right Word

The recentest theory says the extinction of dinosaurs were probably caused by a meteorite who hit the earth.

■ Numbers, Apostrophe (To Form Possessives), Verb (Irregular)

The dinosaurs extinction taked place about 65,000,000 years ago.

■ Subject-Verb Agreement, Plurals, Double Negatives

Some peoples still wonder if there never was no dinosaurs.

WEEK 30: Corrected Sentences

■ Colon, Numbers, Quotation Marks (For Special Words)

Our science class met at 10:30 this morning in the park, and Mr. Bartz showed us the ~~fifty~~ 50 “annual rings” on a cross section of a freshly cut tree.

■ Capitalization, Comma (To Separate Introductory Phrases and Clauses)

After five walks in space, astronauts were able to repair the ~~h~~ Hubble telescope.

■ Subject-Verb Agreement, Adjective (Comparative/Superlative), Using the Right Word

The ~~recentest~~ most recent theory says the extinction of dinosaurs ~~were~~ was probably caused by a meteorite ~~who~~ that hit the earth.

■ Numbers, Apostrophe (To Form Possessives), Verb (Irregular)

The dinosaurs’ extinction ~~taked~~ took place about ~~65,000,000~~ 65 million years ago.

■ Subject-Verb Agreement, Plurals, Double Negatives

Some ~~peoples~~ people still wonder if there ~~never was no~~ ever were any dinosaurs.

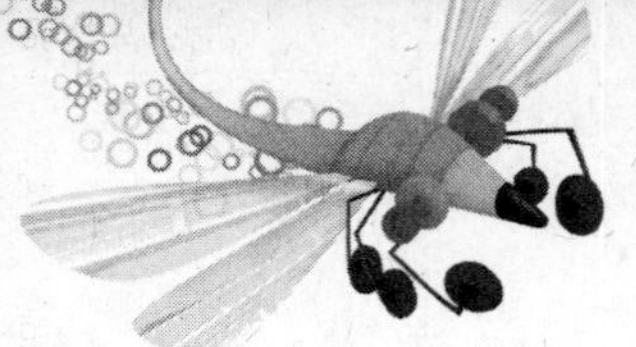

WEEK 31: *Science Facts*

■ Capitalization, Hyphen, Apostrophe (To Form Possessives)

At certain times during the Ice age, one third of the earths surface was covered with ice.

■ Comma (In Addresses), Run-On Sentence, Apostrophe (To Form Possessives)

Glaciers are large rivers of moving ice I have seen pieces break off at the oceans edge to form icebergs near Juneau Alaska.

■ Comma (In Compound Sentences), Subject-Verb Agreement, Apostrophe (In Contractions)

The interior of the earth get hot enough to melt rock and thats how lava are formed.

■ Numbers, Adjective (Comparative/Superlative)

The most oldest rock ever found is over 4,000,000,000 years old!

■ Comma (In Compound Sentences), Adverb (Comparative/Superlative), Plurals

The earth is made of many layeres and the heaviest metals lie more closer to the center.

WEEK 31: Corrected Sentences

■ Capitalization, Hyphen, Apostrophe (To Form Possessives)

At certain times during the Ice ~~age~~ [Age], one[-]third of the earth[']s surface was covered with ice.

■ Comma (In Addresses), Run-On Sentence, Apostrophe (To Form Possessives)

Glaciers are large rivers of moving ice[.] I have seen pieces break off at the ocean[']s edge to form icebergs near Juneau[,] Alaska.

■ Comma (In Compound Sentences), Subject-Verb Agreement, Apostrophe (In Contractions)

The interior of the earth ~~get~~ [gets] hot enough to melt rock[,] and that[']s how lava ~~are~~ [is] formed.

■ Numbers, Adjective (Comparative/Superlative)

The ~~most~~ oldest rock ever found is over ~~4,000,000,000~~ [4 billion] years old!

■ Comma (In Compound Sentences), Adverb (Comparative/Superlative), Plurals

The earth is made of many ~~layeres~~ [layers][,] and the heaviest metals lie ~~more~~ closer to the center.

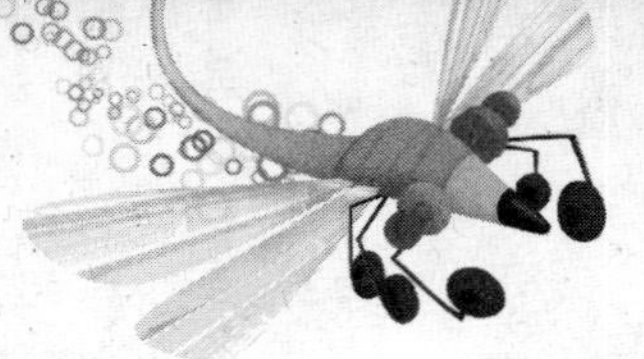

WEEK 32: Inventors and Inventions

■ **Comma (To Set Off Appositives), Abbreviations**

Willis Carrier a scientist from NY invented the first air conditioner.

■ **Hyphen, Comma (To Set Off Appositives and In Addresses)**

The first air conditioned building a movie theater was located in Chicago Illinois.

■ **Using the Right Word, Comma (To Set Off Appositives), Period**

Philo T Farnsworth the father of television invented the electronic device that maid television possible.

■ **Capitalization, Run-On Sentence**

In 1929, Vladimir k. Zworykin invented the first electronic tv system he was a Russian-born american.

■ **Comma (To Set Off Interruptions), Improving Spelling**

The first picture seen on television was beleive it or not Felix the Cat.

WEEK 32: Corrected Sentences

■ Comma (To Set Off Appositives), Abbreviations

New York
Willis Carrier, a scientist from ~~NY~~, invented the first air conditioner.

■ Hyphen, Comma (To Set Off Appositives and In Addresses)

The first air-conditioned building, a movie theater, was located in Chicago, Illinois.

■ Using the Right Word, Comma (To Set Off Appositives), Period

made
Philo T. Farnsworth, the father of television, invented the electronic device that ~~maid~~ television possible.

■ Capitalization, Run-On Sentence

In 1929, Vladimir K. Zworykin invented the first electronic TV system. He was a Russian-born American.

■ Comma (To Set Off Interruptions), Improving Spelling

believe
The first picture seen on television was, ~~beleive~~ it or not, Felix the Cat.

WEEK 33: Story Time

■ Apostrophe (To Form Possessives), Comma (To Set Off Interruptions), Using the Right Word

Sir Gawain in fact ended up being the only night in King Arthurs court who excepted the gigantic Green Knights challenge to battle.

■ Italics and Underlining, Comma (Between Items in a Series), Sentence Fragment

Dickens's book A Christmas Carol about greed change and love.

■ Comma (To Set Off Appositives), Using the Right Word, Italics and Underlining

You wood have liked The Nutcracker the ballet about a girl who dreams of the land of the Sugar Plum Fairy.

■ Quotation Marks, End Punctuation, Pronoun-Antecedent Agreement

Have you read the fairy tale Beauty and the Beast, or have you only seen them as a movie.

■ Comma (To Set Off Appositives), Capitalization, Plurals

Agatha Christie a famous writer of mysterys created the first female detective miss Jane Marple.

WEEK 33: Corrected Sentences

■ Apostrophe (To Form Possessives), Comma (To Set Off Interruptions), Using the Right Word

Sir Gawain, in fact, ended up being the only ~~night~~ knight in King Arthur's court who ~~excepted~~ accepted the gigantic Green Knight's challenge to battle.

■ Italics and Underlining, Comma (Between Items in a Series), Sentence Fragment

Dickens's book <u>A Christmas Carol</u> is about greed, change, and love.

■ Comma (To Set Off Appositives), Using the Right Word, Italics and Underlining

You ~~wood~~ would have liked <u>The Nutcracker</u>, the ballet about a girl who dreams of the land of the Sugar Plum Fairy.

■ Quotation Marks, End Punctuation, Pronoun-Antecedent Agreement

Have you read the fairy tale "Beauty and the Beast," or have you only seen ~~them~~ it as a movie?

■ Comma (To Set Off Appositives), Capitalization, Plurals

Agatha Christie, a famous writer of ~~mysterys~~ mysteries, created the first female detective, Miss Jane Marple.

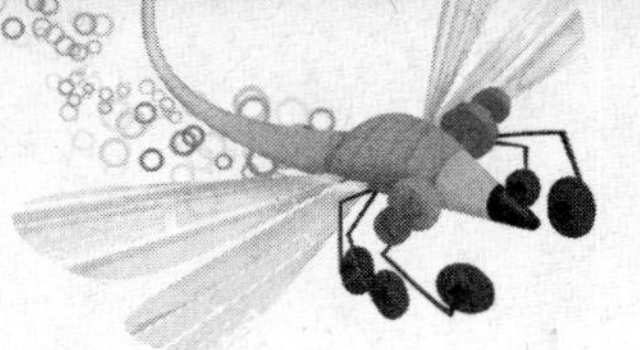

WEEK 34: Literature and Life

■ Comma (To Separate Introductory Phrases and Clauses), Capitalization, Italics and Underlining

In the book harriet the spy Harriet observes and writes about her friends and neighbors in New York City.

■ Comma (In Addresses), Plurals, Italics and Underlining

The book Curious George and all the other storys about this amusing monkey are published by Houghton Mifflin Harcourt 215 Park Avenue South New York NY 10003.

■ Comma (In Dates), Quotation Marks, Period

I said, There are nine birthday cards on the table, and it's 9:00 pm on my special birthday today, September 9 2009!

■ Quotation Marks (For Special Words), Using the Right Word

Humble is the last word that Charlotte rights in her web.

■ Italics and Underlining, Apostrophe (To Form Possessives), Capitalization

Shel Silversteins first book was Lafcadio: the Lion Who Shot Back.

WEEK 34: Corrected Sentences

■ Comma (To Separate Introductory Phrases and Clauses), Capitalization, Italics and Underlining

In the book Harriet the Spy, Harriet observes and writes about her friends and neighbors in New York City.

■ Comma (In Addresses), Plurals, Italics and Underlining

The book Curious George and all the other stories about this amusing monkey are published by Houghton Mifflin Harcourt, 215 Park Avenue South, New York, NY 10003.

■ Comma (In Dates), Quotation Marks, Period

I said, "There are nine birthday cards on the table, and it's 9:00 p.m. on my special birthday today, September 9, 2009!"

■ Quotation Marks (For Special Words), Using the Right Word

"Humble" is the last word that Charlotte writes in her web.

■ Italics and Underlining, Apostrophe (To Form Possessives), Capitalization

Shel Silverstein's first book was Lafcadio: The Lion Who Shot Back.

WEEK 35: Fictional Characters

■ Comma (In Compound Sentences and To Set Off Interruptions)

George and Martha of course are names of a famous couple in history but they are also the names of two hippo friends in a storybook.

■ Hyphen, Quotation Marks, Comma (Between Items in a Series)

A 10 year old Japanese club teaches its members Mother Goose nursery rhymes, such as Little Jack Horner “Little Miss Muffet” and Humpty Dumpty.

■ Apostrophe (To Form Possessives), Subject-Verb Agreement, Italics and Underlining

In Child of the Owl, Caseys Grandmother Paw-Paw live in Chinatown.

■ Using the Right Word, Subject-Verb Agreement, Italics and Underlining

Pippi Longstocking is a book about a spunky girl who can lift a horse and don’t where shoes or like school.

■ Comma (To Separate Introductory Phrases and Clauses), Using the Right Word

When he needed a brake Sherlock Holmes learned himself to play the violin.

WEEK 35: Corrected Sentences

■ Comma (In Compound Sentences and To Set Off Interruptions)

George and Martha, of course, are names of a famous couple in history, but they are also the names of two hippo friends in a storybook.

■ Hyphen, Quotation Marks, Comma (Between Items in a Series)

A 10-year-old Japanese club teaches its members Mother Goose nursery rhymes, such as "Little Jack Horner," "Little Miss Muffet," and "Humpty Dumpty."

■ Apostrophe (To Form Possessives), Subject-Verb Agreement, Italics and Underlining

In Child of the Owl, Casey's Grandmother Paw-Paw ~~live~~ lives in Chinatown.

■ Using the Right Word, Subject-Verb Agreement, Italics and Underlining

Pippi Longstocking is a book about a spunky girl who can lift a horse and ~~don't~~ ~~where~~ doesn't wear shoes or like school.

■ Comma (To Separate Introductory Phrases and Clauses), Using the Right Word

When he needed a ~~brake~~ break, Sherlock Holmes ~~learned~~ taught himself to play the violin.

MUG Shot Paragraphs

The MUG Shot paragraphs are a quick and efficient way to review **m**echanics, **u**sage, and **g**rammar errors each week. These paragraphs can also serve as excellent proofreading exercises. Each paragraph can be corrected and discussed in 8 to 10 minutes.

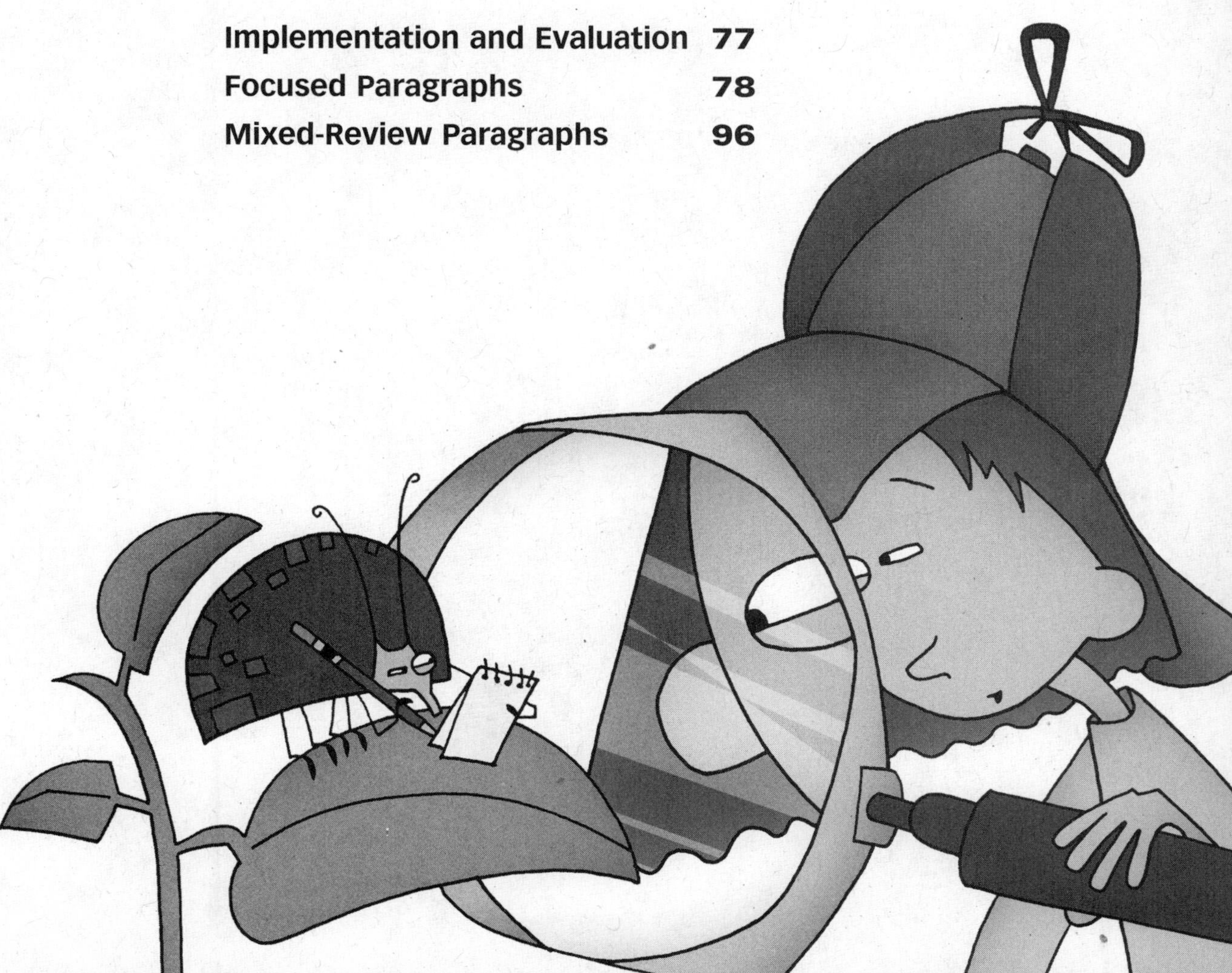

Implementation and Evaluation

For each set of MUG Shot sentences, there is a corresponding MUG Shot paragraph. The first 18 weeks of MUG Shot paragraphs focus on the one or two skills addressed in each week's sentences. The remaining 17 weeks of paragraphs feature a mixed review of proofreading skills addressing select editing and proofreading skills covered in each week's sentences.

Implementation

A MUG Shot paragraph can be implemented at the end of the week as a review or an evaluation activity. It may be done orally as a class. Otherwise you may simply distribute copies of the week's paragraph, read the paragraph aloud, and then have students make their corrections on the sheet. Students may use the "Editing and Proofreading Marks" in their handbooks or on page iv. Have students then discuss their changes (in pairs or in small groups). Afterward, go over the paragraph as a class to make sure that everyone understands the reasons for the changes. (You may want to refer to the corresponding MUG Shot sentences during your discussion.)

An Alternative Approach: Distribute copies of the MUG Shot paragraph along with the edited version. (They appear on the same page in your booklet.) Have students fold the edited version under, and then make their own changes. Once they are finished, they can unfold the paper and check their work.

Evaluation

If you use the paragraphs as an evaluation activity, we recommend that you give students a basic performance score for their work. This score should reflect the number of changes the student has marked correctly (before or after any discussion). The weekly score might also reflect the student's work on the corresponding MUG Shot sentences.

Note: In the MUG Shot paragraphs showing corrections for run-on sentences, sentence fragments, and sentence combining, one possible correction is shown. However, there are often a number of possible answers that would also be correct.

WEEK 1: *California's Name*

■ End Punctuation

What state is named after a character in a book In 1535, the Spanish explorer Cortés came to Baja, California He thought it looked like the beautiful island in a story he had read. The female ruler of the island was named Calafia Ten years later, the area was called California Awesome California was named after a powerful Spanish woman

WEEK 1: Corrected Paragraph

What state is named after a character in a book? In 1535, the Spanish explorer Cortés came to Baja, California. He thought it looked like the beautiful island in a story he had read. The female ruler of the island was named Calafia. Ten years later, the area was called California. Awesome! California was named after a powerful Spanish woman. (or) !

WEEK 2: *If You're an Anteater*

■ Comma (Between Items in a Series)

Anteaters live in Mexico Honduras Panama and other places. They have long heads long tongues and no teeth. Woods swamps and plains are their homes. They eat ants termites and other insects. Their front claws tear open anthills. Then they stick their long tongues into the anthills lick up the insects and eat them. If you're an anteater, you don't mind eating insects for breakfast lunch and dinner.

WEEK 2: Corrected Paragraph

Anteaters live in Mexico, Honduras, Panama, and other places. They have long heads, long tongues, and no teeth. Woods, swamps, and plains are their homes. They eat ants, termites, and other insects. Their front claws tear open anthills. Then they stick their long tongues into the anthills, lick up the insects, and eat them. If you're an anteater, you don't mind eating insects for breakfast, lunch, and dinner.

WEEK 3: Happy Birthday, U.S.A.

■ Comma (In Dates and Addresses)

Independence Day was first celebrated on July 8 1776. The Declaration of Independence was read out loud in Philadelphia Pennsylvania. Church bells rang, people cheered, and bands played. On July 4 1941 the Fourth of July became an official United States holiday. Many people celebrate the Fourth with parades, picnics, and fireworks. All my relatives gather at 101 Center Street Lakewood Iowa every year for a great family picnic. We have a sack race, an egg toss, and some volleyball games.

WEEK 3: Corrected Paragraph

Independence Day was first celebrated on July 8, 1776. The Declaration of Independence was read out loud in Philadelphia, Pennsylvania. Church bells rang, people cheered, and bands played. On July 4, 1941, the Fourth of July became an official United States holiday. Many people celebrate the Fourth with parades, picnics, and fireworks. All my relatives gather at 101 Center Street, Lakewood, Iowa, every year for a great family picnic. We have a sack race, an egg toss, and some volleyball games.

WEEK 4: Rain, Rain, *Go* Away

■ Comma (To Keep Numbers Clear and To Set Off Interjections)

Who gets the most rain? Well in the United States it's the Southeast. Some places there get around 1778 millimeters a year (that's 70 inches). The average yearly rainfall in northeastern India is 10922 millimeters (that's about 430 inches). Wow the Philippines holds the record for the most rain in one day. During a typhoon, they got nearly 1168 millimeters (almost 46 inches)!

WEEK 4: Corrected Paragraph

Who gets the most rain? Well‸, in the United States it's the Southeast. Some places there get around 1‸,778 millimeters a year (that's 70 inches). The average yearly rainfall in northeastern India is 10‸,922 millimeters (that's about 430 inches). Wow‸, the Philippines holds the record for the most rain in one day. During a typhoon, they got nearly 1‸,168 millimeters (almost 46 inches)!

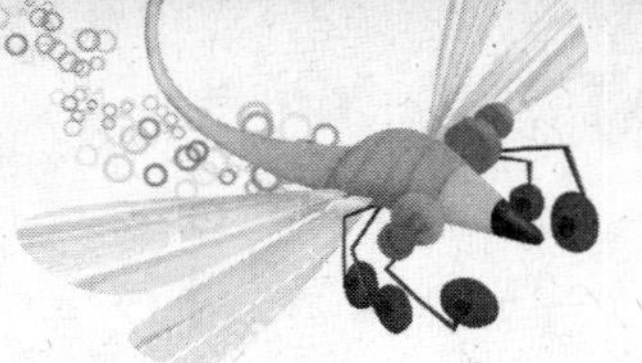

WEEK 5: Mt. McKinley First

■ Comma (In Compound Sentences)

The highest mountain in North America is Mt. McKinley in Alaska but its Native American name is *Denali.* The word *Denali* means "High One" and it is. Mt. McKinley is 20,320 feet high. Rev. Hudson Stuck led a four-man team to the top in 1913. Walter Harper, a Native American from Alaska, got there first but the others were right behind him. The men were on top of the world and they were very thankful to be safe.

WEEK 5: Corrected Paragraph

The highest mountain in North America is Mt. McKinley in Alaska, but its Native American name is *Denali.* The word *Denali* means "High One," and it is. Mt. McKinley is 20,320 feet high. Rev. Hudson Stuck led a four-man team to the top in 1913. Walter Harper, a Native American from Alaska, got there first, but the others were right behind him. The men were on top of the world, and they were very thankful to be safe.

WEEK 6: Football Fans

■ Hyphen

While one half of our family stays home, my dad and I zip off to the football game. In our town, most games have sellout crowds. We arrive two hours early to find an on site parking space. We wave to fun loving fans. Then we climb to our upper deck seats. The bone chilling wind whips around us in our nosebleed seats. We don't care. We are "all American" football fans!

WEEK 6: Corrected Paragraph

While one-half of our family stays home, my dad and I zip off to the football game. In our town, most games have sellout crowds. We arrive two hours early to find an on-site parking space. We wave to fun-loving fans. Then we climb to our upper-deck seats. The bone-chilling wind whips around us in our nosebleed seats. We don't care. We are "all-American" football fans!

WEEK 7: *Good Books*

■ Apostrophe (In Contractions and To Form Possessives)

Have you ever read a book that you couldnt put down? Two popular childrens books are *Charlottes Web* and *Dear Mr. Henshaw.* Theyre not new books, but theyre both best sellers. Kids havent stopped reading them. With these books, maybe youll laugh or maybe youll cry. Youll feel and think about what youve read. Thats one reason why some books dont get dusty.

WEEK 7: Corrected Paragraph

Have you ever read a book that you couldn't put down? Two popular children's books are *Charlotte's Web* and *Dear Mr. Henshaw.* They're not new books, but they're both best sellers. Kids haven't stopped reading them. With these books, maybe you'll laugh or maybe you'll cry. You'll feel and think about what you've read. That's one reason why some books don't get dusty.

WEEK 8: *Girl with the Crooked Hair*

■ Quotation Marks

Writer Sandra Cisneros wrote a short story called Eleven. She said, When I think how I see myself, I would have to be at age 11. I know I'm 32 on the outside, but inside I'm 11. When she was young, her family traveled between Chicago and Mexico. I didn't like school because we moved so much, she said. Another problem was her looks. She said, I'm the girl in the picture with skinny arms and a crumpled shirt and crooked hair. Today, Cisneros is a well-known writer.

WEEK 8: Corrected Paragraph

Writer Sandra Cisneros wrote a short story called "Eleven." She said, "When I think how I see myself, I would have to be at age 11. I know I'm 32 on the outside, but inside I'm 11." When she was young, her family traveled between Chicago and Mexico. "I didn't like school because we moved so much," she said. Another problem was her looks. She said, "I'm the girl in the picture with skinny arms and a crumpled shirt and crooked hair." Today, Cisneros is a well-known writer.

WEEK 9: The Real McCoy

■ Capitalization

Elijah McCoy was born before the civil war ended. his mother and father were ex-slaves. they escaped to canada on the underground railroad. later they returned to the united states. their son, elijah, went to scotland to study Engineering. when he returned, no one would hire an african american engineer. in spite of that, Elijah McCoy became a famous inventor. when people wanted a particular invention of McCoy's, they asked for the "real McCoy."

WEEK 9: Corrected Paragraph

Elijah McCoy was born before the civil war ended. his mother and father were ex-slaves. they escaped to canada on the underground railroad. later they returned to the united states. their son, elijah, went to scotland to study Engineering. when he returned, no one would hire an african american engineer. in spite of that, Elijah McCoy became a famous inventor. when people wanted a particular invention of McCoy's, they asked for the "real McCoy."

WEEK 10: The Perfect Vacation

■ Capitalization

For a perfect vacation, would you go west to the rockies or east to the appalachian mountains? how about kicking around in the atlantic ocean or the gulf of mexico? Do you dream of going to yellowstone national park, niagara falls, or the grand canyon? How about a trip to europe or africa? If you want to fly to the Moon, you'll have to wait a few years.

WEEK 10: Corrected Paragraph

R
For a perfect vacation, would you go west to the rockies or east to
A M H A
the appalachian mountains? how about kicking around in the atlantic
O G M Y
ocean or the gulf of mexico? Do you dream of going to yellowstone
N P N F G C
national park, niagara falls, or the grand canyon? How about a trip to
E A m
europe or africa? If you want to fly to the Moon, you'll have to wait a
few years.

WEEK 11: Looking at Art

■ Plurals

The buses dropped us off at the art museum. Four bronze horsemans guarded the entrance. They had swords and knifes. Angeles with halos were painted on the ceiling. Our guide led us through rooms called gallerys. Paintings of tables piled with food started making us hungry. Later, we ate box lunchs. Inside were sandwichs or tacos, a couple spoonsful of fruit salad, with big blueberrys and bright red cherrys.

WEEK 11: Corrected Paragraph

The buses dropped us off at the art museum. Four bronze ~~horsemans~~ horsemen guarded the entrance. They had swords and ~~knifes~~ knives. ~~Angeles~~ Angels with halos were painted on the ceiling. Our guide led us through rooms called ~~gallerys~~ galleries. Paintings of tables piled with food started making us hungry. Later, we ate box ~~lunchs~~ lunches. Inside were ~~sandwichs~~ sandwiches or tacos, a couple ~~spoonsful~~ spoonfuls of fruit salad, with big ~~blueberrys~~ blueberries and bright red ~~cherrys~~ cherries.

WEEK 12: The First Americans

■ Numbers

20,000 years ago, the first people probably wandered into North and South America from northeast Asia. Nearly 1,000,000 Native Americans were living in the United States when Columbus "discovered" them. By nineteen ten, wars, sickness, and starvation left only 220 thousand Native Americans. 2,000,000 Native Americans live in the United States today. They are not 1 people, but many different peoples with their own histories and ways of life.

WEEK 12: Corrected Paragraph

~~20,000~~ Twenty thousand years ago, the first people probably wandered into North and South America from northeast Asia. Nearly ~~1,000,000~~ 1 million Native Americans were living in the United States when Columbus "discovered" them. By ~~nineteen ten~~ 1910, wars, sickness, and starvation left only ~~220 thousand~~ 220,000 Native Americans. ~~2,000,000~~ Two million Native Americans live in the United States today. They are not ~~1~~ one people, but many different peoples with their own histories and ways of life.

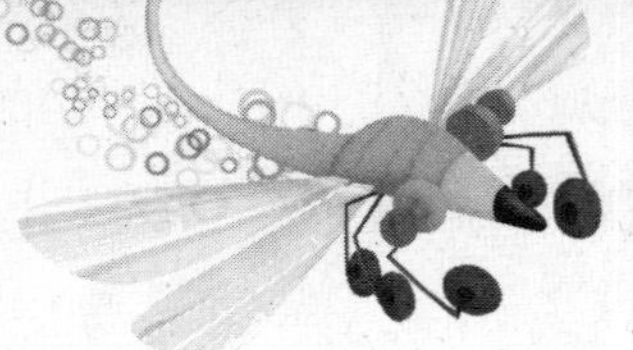

WEEK 13: *Tornado Watch*

■ Subject-Verb Agreement

What causes a tornado? A "front" form between a cold air mass and a warm air mass. Sometimes a cold air mass move in above the warm air. The hot air rises. It spins. Then it form a funnel-shaped cloud—a tornado. Weather experts looks for these conditions. Then they gives a "tornado watch." The winds inside a tornado may reach 500 miles per hour. Sometimes a tornado touch the ground and destroy everything in its way.

WEEK 13: Corrected Paragraph

What causes a tornado? A "front" ~~form~~ forms between a cold air mass and a warm air mass. Sometimes a cold air mass ~~move~~ moves in above the warm air. The hot air rises. It spins. Then it ~~form~~ forms a funnel-shaped cloud—a tornado. Weather experts ~~looks~~ look for these conditions. Then they ~~gives~~ give a "tornado watch." The winds inside a tornado may reach 500 miles per hour. Sometimes a tornado ~~touch~~ touches the ground and ~~destroy~~ destroys everything in its way.

WEEK 14: "*Oh, Give Me a Home . . .*"

■ Subject-Verb Agreement

Where does the deer and the antelope play? One place is Yellowstone National Park. It were created in 1872. Parts of the park is in Wyoming, Montana, and Idaho. The park are a safe place for many animals. Bears, moose, buffalo, deer, and antelope lives there. Beavers, otters, fish, and eagles also enjoys the park. For them, Yellowstone be "home sweet home."

WEEK 14: Corrected Paragraph

Where ~~does~~ do the deer and the antelope play? One place is Yellowstone National Park. It ~~were~~ was created in 1872. Parts of the park ~~is~~ are in Wyoming, Montana, and Idaho. The park ~~are~~ is a safe place for many animals. Bears, moose, buffalo, deer, and antelope ~~lives~~ live there. Beavers, otters, fish, and eagles also ~~enjoys~~ enjoy the park. For them, Yellowstone ~~be~~ is "home sweet home."

WEEK 15: Ding-dong! Crack!

■ Run-On Sentence

Have you ever seen the Liberty Bell it's big, it's old, and it's cracked. The Liberty Bell weighs 2,000 pounds it was around when the United States was still a baby. It rang out to signal holidays, meetings, and fire alarms. It cracked the first time it was used then it was fixed. Many years later, it cracked again this time it could not be fixed. The old bell is on display near Independence Hall in Philadelphia it no longer rings, but it's still the bell of freedom.

WEEK 15: Corrected Paragraph

Have you ever seen the Liberty Bell? It's big, it's old, and it's cracked. The Liberty Bell weighs 2,000 pounds. It was around when the United States was still a baby. It rang out to signal holidays, meetings, and fire alarms. It cracked the first time it was used. Then it was fixed. Many years later, it cracked again. This time it could not be fixed. The old bell is on display near Independence Hall in Philadelphia. It no longer rings, but it's still the bell of freedom.

WEEK 16: Everybody Has Rights

Sentence Fragment

Dorothea Dix. Born in Maine in 1802. She taught school for many years. Then volunteered to teach a Sunday school class in a prison. What she found was shocking. Mental patients. Shared prison cells with criminals and were treated worse than animals. Wrote a long report. Mental patients not being criminals. Many things changed because of Dorothea Dix.

WEEK 16: Corrected Paragraph

Dorothea Dix. was Born in Maine in 1802. She taught school for many years. Then she volunteered to teach a Sunday school class in a prison. What she found was shocking. Mental patients. Shared prison cells with criminals and were treated worse than animals. Dorothea Wrote a long report. about m Mental patients not being criminals. Many things changed because of Dorothea Dix.

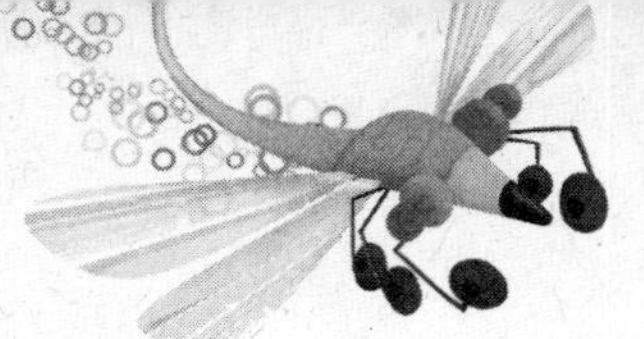

WEEK 17: Hey, Pick That Up!

■ Using the Right Word

Does it matter what you do with you're trash? Yes, it does! You no how you run out of things at home. Earth could run out of things, to. It could run out of clean air and fresh water. But there are alot of ways to help. Sit up a recycling program at your school, or right an article four your school paper. Bring bottles, newspapers, and aluminum cans to a recycling center. Learn others what to do. You *can* have a positive affect.

WEEK 17: Corrected Paragraph

Does it matter what you do with ~~you're~~ your trash? Yes, it does! You ~~no~~ know how you run out of things at home. Earth could run out of things, ~~to~~ too. It could run out of clean air and fresh water. But there are ~~alot~~ a lot of ways to help. ~~Sit~~ Set up a recycling program at your school, or ~~right~~ write an article ~~four~~ for your school paper. ~~Bring~~ Take bottles, newspapers, and aluminum cans to a recycling center. ~~Learn~~ Teach others what to do. You *can* have a positive ~~affect~~ effect.

WEEK 18: The Nearest Planet

■ Combining Sentences

Did you ever look for Venus in the sky? Did you ever look for Venus in the evening? Venus is a planet. Venus is a bright planet. It is between Earth and Mercury. It reflects the sun's light. It has no light of its own. Its environment is red-hot. Its environment would burn you to a crisp if you were there. Venus has pools of liquid metal. Venus has clouds of liquid acid. It has lightning storms. It has erupting volcanoes.

WEEK 18: Corrected Paragraph

Did you ever look for Venus in the evening sky? ~~Did you ever look for Venus in the evening?~~ Venus is a bright planet~~.~~ ~~Venus is a bright planet. It is~~ between Earth and Mercury. It reflects the sun's light, but ~~I~~it has no light of its own. Its red-hot environment ~~is red-hot. Its environment~~ would burn you to a crisp if you were there. Venus has pools of liquid metal, and ~~Venus has~~ clouds of liquid acid. It has lightning storms, and ~~It has~~ erupting volcanoes.

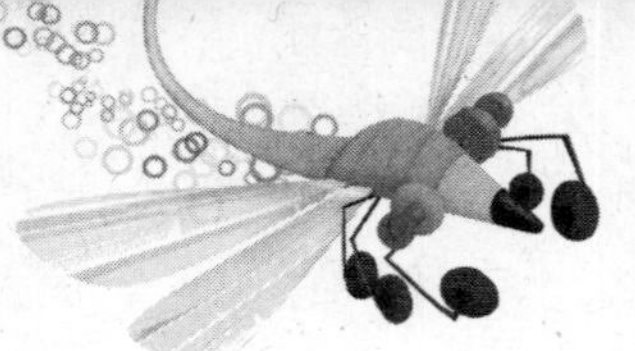

WEEK 19: Fingers Do the Talking

■ Using the Right Word, Verb (Irregular), Run-On Sentence

The Plains Indians of North America belonged to many different tribes they speaked many different languages. How could they communicate? They used their hands to make signs for creeks, rivers, and fir trees. White men wore hats the sign for a white man showed a hat. Sum signs had several meanings. If an Indian pretended to shiver, that could have meant cold it could also have meant winter whether. Sign language is a creative way of talking.

WEEK 19: Corrected Paragraph

The Plains Indians of North America belonged to many different tribes. They ~~speaked~~ spoke many different languages. How could they communicate? They used their hands to make signs for creeks, rivers, and fir trees. White men wore hats, so the sign for a white man showed a hat. ~~Sum~~ Some signs had several meanings. If an Indian pretended to shiver, that could have meant cold. It could also have meant winter ~~whether~~ weather. Sign language is a creative way of talking.

WEEK 20: *Spelling Challenge*

■ Comma (Between Items in a Series), Pronoun-Antecedent Agreement, Subject-Verb Agreement, Capitalization

Where is English spoken? The countries includes the United States, the United kingdom, Canada, Australia new Zealand and south africa. English have the largest vocabulary in the world. It has "borrowed" words from European, Arabic African and asian languages. Many English words are hard to spell. It is often not spelled the way it sounds (*night, through,* and *reign*).

WEEK 20: Corrected Paragraph

Where is English spoken? The countries ~~includes~~ include the United States, the United ~~k~~ K ingdom, Canada, Australia, ~~n~~ N ew Zealand, and ~~s~~ S outh ~~a~~ A frica. English ~~have~~ has the largest vocabulary in the world. It has "borrowed" words from European, Arabic, African, and ~~a~~ A sian languages. Many English words are hard to spell. ~~It is~~ They are often not spelled the way ~~it sounds~~ they sound (*night, through,* and *reign*).

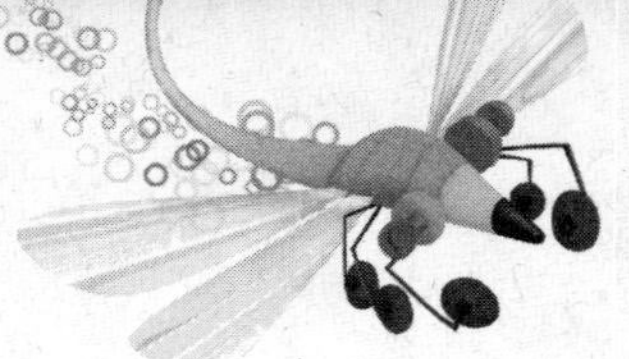

WEEK 21: Fishy Facts

■ Adjective (Comparative/Superlative), Pronoun-Antecedent Agreement, Comma (To Set Off Interjections), Numbers, Semicolon

The following facts might sound fishy to you, but it's true. Atlantic salmon can leap fifteen feet into the air. Yes but that's a small distance compared to flying fish. They don't actually fly they glide through the air. They can travel more than ninety feet if they're being chased. The most fast fish of all is the sailfish. It has been clocked at sixty miles per hour. Say that's fast enough to get a speeding ticket.

WEEK 21: Corrected Paragraph

The following facts might sound fishy to you, but ~~it's~~ they're true. Atlantic salmon can leap ~~fifteen~~ 15 feet into the air. Yes, but that's a small distance compared to flying fish. They don't actually fly; they glide through the air. They can travel more than ~~ninety~~ 90 feet if they're being chased. The ~~most fast~~ fastest fish of all is the sailfish. It has been clocked at ~~sixty~~ 60 miles per hour. Say, that's fast enough to get a speeding ticket.

WEEK 22: *Good Dog*

■ Comma (Between Items in a Series), Hyphen, Rambling Sentence, Colon

The poodle is a popular breed of dog in the United States and poodles tend to be intelligent and they are good with kids. Some of the following dogs make good pets golden retrievers Labradors and collies. They are all friendly playful and good natured dogs. You should talk to your dog walk your dog and teach your dog to lie down. If you treat your dog well, you will have a friend for life.

WEEK 22: Corrected Paragraph

The poodle is a popular breed of dog in the United States. Poodles tend to be intelligent, and they are good with kids. Some of the following dogs make good pets: golden retrievers, Labradors, and collies. They are all friendly, playful, and good-natured dogs. You should talk to your dog, walk your dog, and teach your dog to lie down. If you treat your dog well, you will have a friend for life.

WEEK 23: The Gulf Stream

■ Comma (In Direct Address), Improving Spelling, Capitalization, Apostrophe (In Contractions)

"Students on a map of the United States, you will see a 'finger' in the southeast. Thats the peninsula called florida. It separates the gulf of mexico from the atlantic ocean. The Gulf Stream, a powerful, warm-water current, moves like a river within the ocean. it flows northeast arround Florida. Find the united kingdom on a world map. It has a higher latitude than Maine, but its much warmer. the Gulf Stream warms it up."

WEEK 23: Corrected Paragraph

"Students on a map of the United States, you will see a 'finger' in
        S   ,   '   F   G
the southeast. Thats the peninsula called florida. It separates the gulf of
M   A   O
mexico from the atlantic ocean. The Gulf Stream, a powerful, warm-water
                                                  I   around
current, moves like a river within the ocean. it flows northeast ~~arround~~
                            U   K
Florida. Find the united kingdom on a world map. It has a higher
                                        '   T
latitude than Maine, but its much warmer. the Gulf Stream warms it up."

WEEK 24: Look at Minnesota

■ Italics and Underlining, Comma (To Keep Numbers Clear), Capitalization

About 60000 of Minnesota's 5100958 people are native americans. The name of the state comes from a Sioux word. It means "many-tinted waters." Two famous minnesotans are Judy Garland and Charles Lindbergh. They took trips everyone remembers, but they didn't start from their home state. Judy Garland as Dorothy traveled from Kansas to oz in the movie The wizard of Oz. Charles Lindbergh flew the first solo Airplane flight from New York to Paris in 1927.

WEEK 24: Corrected Paragraph

About 60000 of Minnesota's 5100958 people are native americans. The name of the state comes from a Sioux word. It means "many-tinted waters." Two famous minnesotans are Judy Garland and Charles Lindbergh. They took trips everyone remembers, but they didn't start from their home state. Judy Garland as Dorothy traveled from Kansas to oz in the movie The wizard of Oz. Charles Lindbergh flew the first solo Airplane flight from New York to Paris in 1927.

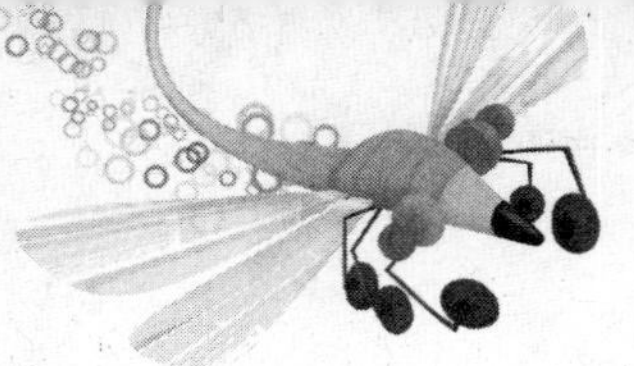

WEEK 25: Hot Spots

■ **Capitalization, Comma (To Separate Equal Adjectives), Semicolon, Using the Right Word**

Although a dessert may be hot or cold, it is always dry. Deserts cover about one-fifth of the earth. The biggest desert in north america is the sonoran desert. Death valley is alot smaller it is scarier. It is the hottest driest place in north America. The gold miners in 1849 past through Death Valley. They were unprepared. Many didn't have enough food or water, so many hungry thirsty miners dyed in that desert.

WEEK 25: Corrected Paragraph

Although a ~~dessert~~ desert may be hot or cold, it is always dry. Deserts cover about one-fifth of the earth. The biggest desert in ~~n~~North ~~a~~America is the ~~s~~Sonoran ~~d~~Desert. Death ~~v~~Valley is ~~alot~~ a lot smaller; it is scarier. It is the hottest, driest place in ~~n~~North America. The gold miners in 1849 ~~past~~ passed through Death Valley. They were unprepared. Many didn't have enough food or water, so many hungry, thirsty miners ~~dyed~~ died in that desert.

WEEK 26: *Don't Step on Me*

■ Quotation Marks, Sentence Fragment, Comma (To Set Off Dialogue), Using the Right Word

One early American flag a rattlesnake printed on it. The flag had this motto "Don't tread on me. That's another way of saying "Don't step on me. When the 13 colonies became the United States. They made a new flag. It had 13 stripes. And 13 stars in a circle. That worked good until knew states came on the seen. Then it was decided to add a new star four every new state. The last pare of stars was added in 1959 for Alaska and Hawaii.

WEEK 26: Corrected Paragraph

One early American flag had a rattlesnake printed on it. The flag had this motto "Don't tread on me." That's another way of saying "Don't step on me." When the 13 colonies became the United States, They made a new flag. It had 13 stripes, And 13 stars in a circle. That worked ~~good~~ well until ~~knew~~ new states came on the ~~seen~~ scene. Then it was decided to add a new star ~~four~~ for every new state. The last ~~pare~~ pair of stars was added in 1959 for Alaska and Hawaii.

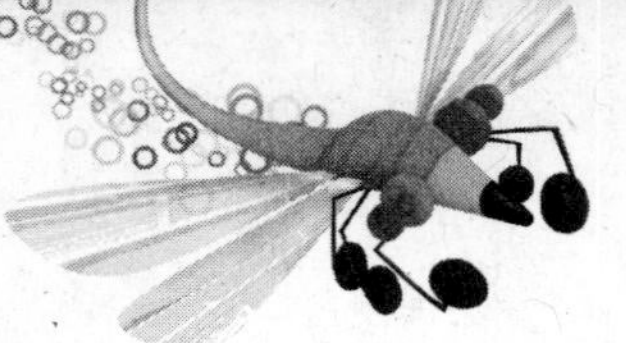

WEEK 27: Safety Engineers

■ Comma (To Separate Equal Adjectives), Verb (Irregular), Capitalization, and End Punctuation

You have probably heared the saying, "An ounce of prevention is worth a pound of cure." Did you know that there are safety engineers who figure out what can go wrong. They look at things like machines, factories, and roads. Does a machine have a sharp uncovered moving part. Workers could get hurt. Is there a super-sharp turn drivers could run off the road. Safety engineers work on ways to avoid accidents

WEEK 27: Corrected Paragraph

You have probably ~~heared~~ heard the saying, "An ounce of prevention is worth a pound of cure." Did you know that there are safety engineers who figure out what can go wrong? They look at things like machines, factories, and roads. Does a machine have a sharp, uncovered, moving part? Workers could get hurt. Is there a super-sharp turn? Drivers could run off the road. Safety engineers work on ways to avoid accidents.

WEEK 28: *Powerful Words*

Comma (To Keep Numbers Clear and To Separate Introductory Phrases and Clauses), Quotation Marks, Italics and Underlining

Born in England in 1737 Thomas Paine eventually came to America as an adult and then started to write about freedom. He published a little book called Common Sense. It sold more than 500000 copies. The birthday of a new world is at hand, Paine said. A general named George Washington read Paine's words to the troops at Trenton. After hearing the reading the soldiers were inspired, attacked the British, and won. It was a turning point in the Revolutionary War.

WEEK 28: Corrected Paragraph

Born in England in 1737, Thomas Paine eventually came to America as an adult and then started to write about freedom. He published a little book called Common Sense. It sold more than 500,000 copies. "The birthday of a new world is at hand," Paine said. A general named George Washington read Paine's words to the troops at Trenton. After hearing the reading, the soldiers were inspired, attacked the British, and won. It was a turning point in the Revolutionary War.

WEEK 29: Flags over Florida

■ Comma (In Compound Sentences), Capitalization, Numbers, Verb (Irregular)

In 1698, Spain had a colony in pensacola, florida. In 1719, the french fighted and pushed out the spanish for 3 years. Then the Spanish took over again. Next came the british in 1763. They ruled for twenty years but then the Spanish took over again. Britain controlled pensacola during the war of 1812. In 1814, Pensacola was captured by United States forces. Then Spain recaptured the city for 1 last time. Finally, florida became a state in 1821 and Pensacola became part of the United States.

WEEK 29: Corrected Paragraph

In 1698, Spain had a colony in ~~p~~Pensacola, ~~f~~Florida. In 1719, the ~~f~~French ~~fighted~~ fought and pushed out the ~~s~~Spanish for ~~3~~ three years. Then the Spanish took over again. Next came the ~~b~~British in 1763. They ruled for ~~twenty~~ 20 years, but then the Spanish took over again. Britain controlled ~~p~~Pensacola during the ~~w~~War of 1812. In 1814, Pensacola was captured by United States forces. Then Spain recaptured the city for ~~1~~ one last time. Finally, ~~f~~Florida became a state in 1821, and Pensacola became part of the United States.

WEEK 30: When Dinosaurs Ruled

■ Quotation Marks (For Special Words), Plurals, Double Negatives, Adjective (Comparative/Superlative)

The word *dinosaur* means “terrible lizard. Dinosaurs weren't never really lizards. And they weren't really terrible. Many dinosaurs had big bodys and small brains. Some dinosaurs were plant eaters, and some were meat eaters. One of the most large plant eaters was Seismosaurus (131 feets long). The biggest meat eater was Giganotosaurus (49 feets long). Dinosaurs ruled the earth for 100 million years and then disappeared.

WEEK 30: Corrected Paragraph

The word *dinosaur* means “terrible lizard.” Dinosaurs weren't ~~never~~ really lizards. And they weren't really terrible. Many dinosaurs had big bodies ~~bodys~~ and small brains. Some dinosaurs were plant eaters, and some were meat eaters. One of the largest ~~most large~~ plant eaters was Seismosaurus (131 feet ~~feets~~ long). The biggest meat eater was Giganotosaurus (49 feet ~~feets~~ long). Dinosaurs ruled the earth for 100 million years and then disappeared.

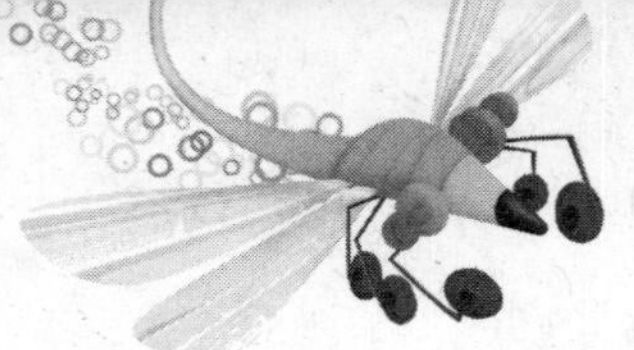

WEEK 31: *Deep Space*

■ Capitalization, Comma (In Addresses), Run-On Sentence, Adverb (Comparative/Superlative)

People once thought that earth was the center of the universe. Now we know more better. Once we believed our galaxy was the only one in the universe we were wrong about that, too. A galaxy is a collection of stars, planets, and space dust. Our galaxy is called the milky way there are billions of galaxies. In the 1920s, Edwin Hubble, an american astronomer, proved that. The hubble telescope in Palomar California is named after him.

WEEK 31: Corrected Paragraph

People once thought that Earth was the center of the universe. Now we know ~~more~~ better. Once we believed our galaxy was the only one in the universe, but we were wrong about that, too. A galaxy is a collection of stars, planets, and space dust. Our galaxy is called the Milky Way. There are billions of galaxies. In the 1920s, Edwin Hubble, an American astronomer, proved that. The Hubble telescope in Palomar, California, is named after him.

WEEK 32: Watch the Best, Shut Off the Rest

■ Comma (To Set Off Appositives and Interruptions), Abbreviations, Run-On Sentence, Hyphen

Some families have television viewing rules some parents let their kids watch only public television and kids' shows. Some keep the television turned off on school nights. There's junk on tv however there's good stuff, too. Cooking and drawing shows for example teach you something. Other shows field trip or interview programs answer questions about everything from movie special effects to life on aircraft carriers. Parents and kids can make well informed choices.

WEEK 32: Corrected Paragraph

Some families have television viewing rules some parents let their kids watch only public television and kids' shows. Some keep the television turned off on school nights. There's junk on tv however there's good stuff, too. Cooking and drawing shows for example teach you something. Other shows field trip or interview programs answer questions about everything from movie special effects to life on aircraft carriers. Parents and kids can make well informed choices.

WEEK 33: A King from Camelot

■ Pronoun-Antecedent Agreement, Comma (To Set Off Interruptions), Plurals, End Punctuation

Do you like tales of knights in shining armor. Do you love beautiful ladys-in-waiting. If you said yes and hopefully you did you'll enjoy *The Legend of King Arthur*. A legend is partly true and partly made up. There probably was a British leader long ago named Arthur. We don't know much about them. We do however have storys about the *legendary* King Arthur and his reign in a kingdom called Camelot

WEEK 33: Corrected Paragraph

Do you like tales of knights in shining armor? Do you love beautiful ~~ladys~~ ladies-in-waiting? If you said yes, and hopefully you did, you'll enjoy *The Legend of King Arthur*. A legend is partly true and partly made up. There probably was a British leader long ago named Arthur. We don't know much about ~~them~~ him. We do, however, have ~~storys~~ stories about the *legendary* King Arthur and his reign in a kingdom called Camelot.

WEEK 34: He Let His Light Shine

■ Comma (In Dates and Addresses), Quotation Marks, Plurals, Period, Italics and Underlining

This is how the writer Shel Silverstein described his childhood: “I couldn’t play ball, I couldn’t dance, luckily, the girls didn’t want me, so I started to draw and to write. His first hit was the book The Giving Tree. He also wrote Where the Sidewalk Ends. His books have sold more than 14 million copys. Mr Silverstein died on May 10 1999 in Key West Florida. The world has lost a wonderful writer.

WEEK 34: Corrected Paragraph

This is how the writer Shel Silverstein described his childhood: “I couldn’t play ball, I couldn’t dance, luckily, the girls didn’t want me, so I started to draw and to write.” His first hit was the book <u>The Giving Tree</u>. He also wrote <u>Where the Sidewalk Ends</u>. His books have sold more than 14 million ~~copys~~ copies. Mr. Silverstein died on May 10, 1999, in Key West, Florida. The world has lost a wonderful writer.

WEEK 35: Mother *Goose* in Japan

■ Quotation Marks, Subject-Verb Agreement, Using the Right Word, Comma (Between Items in a Series)

Can you recite Mary Had a Little Lamb? Mother Goose rhymes is not just four kids. They're great for people learning English, to. Yasui Sadao is a high-school English teacher in Japan. He uses Mother Goose poems to teach his students English. Japan even has a Mother Goose Society. The society has it's own Web site newsletter study group and yearly national meeting.

WEEK 35: Corrected Paragraph

Can you recite "Mary Had a Little Lamb?" Mother Goose rhymes ~~is~~ are not just ~~four~~ for kids. They're great for people learning English, ~~to~~ too. Yasui Sadao is a high-school English teacher in Japan. He uses Mother Goose poems to teach his students English. Japan even has a Mother Goose Society. The society has ~~it's~~ its own Web site, newsletter, study group, and yearly national meeting.

Daily Writing Practice

This section offers three types of exercises. **Writing prompts** are sentences and pictures designed to inspire freewriting (which students may share in class and later shape into finished narratives or essays). **Writing topics** address a wide range of writing ideas. Finally, the **Show-Me sentences** provide practice in developing the important skill of "showing" in writing.

Writing Prompts

A Writing Prompts FAQ Sheet

You may duplicate the following question-and-answer information about writing prompts as a handout for students or use it as the basis for a class discussion.

Anyone who wants to be a good writer has to practice often. That's why so many writers keep journals and diaries. And that's why your teacher asks you to write something nearly every day in school. Your teacher may ask you to write about a specific topic or about a personal experience. Your teacher might also ask you to use a writing prompt.

A writing prompt can be anything from a question to a photograph to a quotation. The idea is for you to write whatever you can without planning or researching the topic. You simply write what you have inside. And you keep writing until all your thoughts are gone. That's it!

How do I get started? It's really very simple. You just write down whatever comes into your mind when you think about your writing prompt. This doesn't have to be much. All you are looking for is an idea to get you going.

Shouldn't I plan out what I'm going to write about? No, you shouldn't plan anything. That's the whole idea. Just write. You don't need to know where your writing will take you. Mystery is good; in fact, it is the mystery and surprises along the way that get writers hooked on writing.

How can I keep my writing going? Don't stop! When you run out of ideas, shift gears and try writing about your topic in a slightly different way. For example, you might compare your topic to something else. Or you might use dialogue between two or more people who are discussing your topic. Or you might think of a specific audience—like a group of first graders—and write so they can understand your topic. Whatever you do, keep the ideas flowing as freely as possible.

When should I stop? If you are doing a timed writing (3, 5, or 10 minutes), stop when the time is up. You might decide it's time to stop when you've filled up the entire page. (Or you might keep going, using another sheet of paper.) Or you might decide to stop when you feel that you've done as much thinking and writing as you can and your brain is drained.

What do I do with my writing? You might share it with a classmate and see what she or he thinks. Or you might turn your writing into a more polished essay, story, or poem. Or you might set it aside and use it later when you need a topic for a writing assignment.

So, really, all I have to do is start writing? Right!

WRITING PROMPT

I want to learn to play the . . .

WRITING PROMPT

Life in the Sea

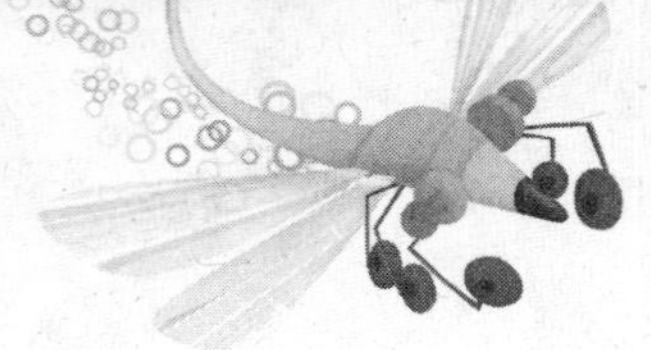

WRITING PROMPT

The tiger was staring right at me.

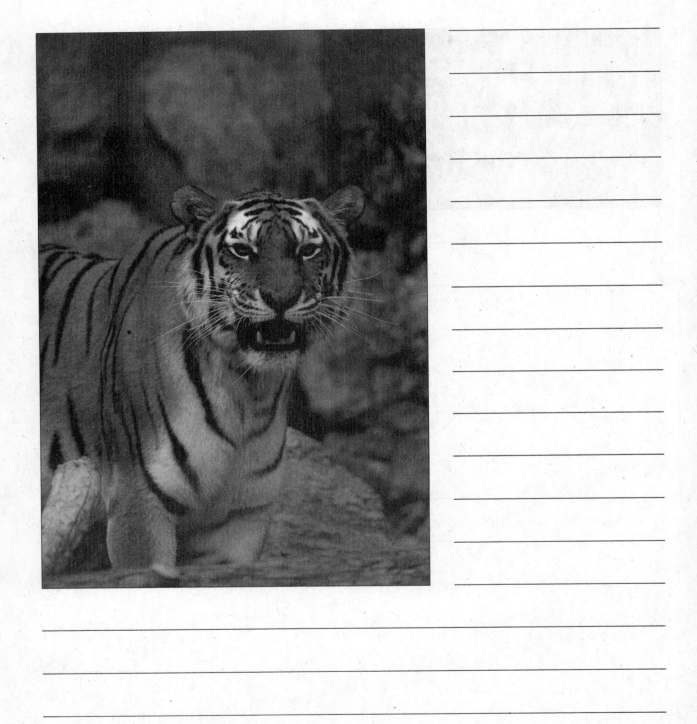

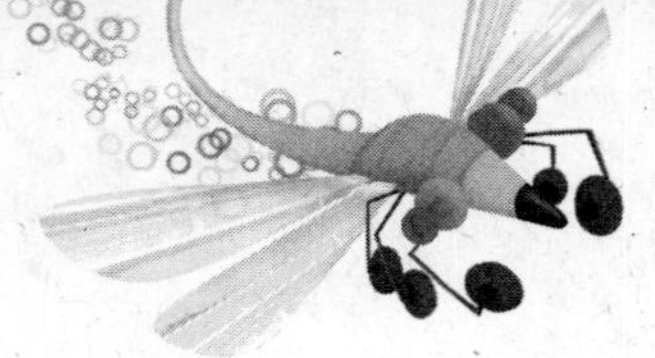

WRITING PROMPT

In the Middle of the Park

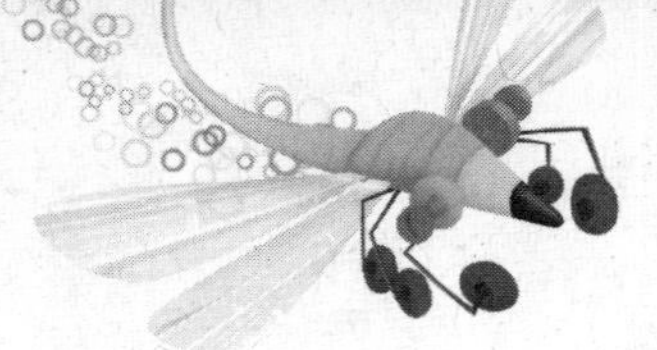

WRITING PROMPT

One little banana peel on the floor was all it took . . .

WRITING PROMPT

Someplace I'd really like to visit . . .

WRITING PROMPT

Uh-*oh*!

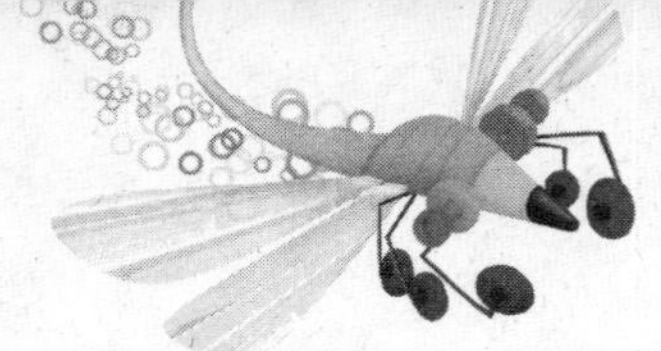

WRITING PROMPT

Someone dropped a wallet.

WRITING PROMPT

I couldn't believe my eyes!

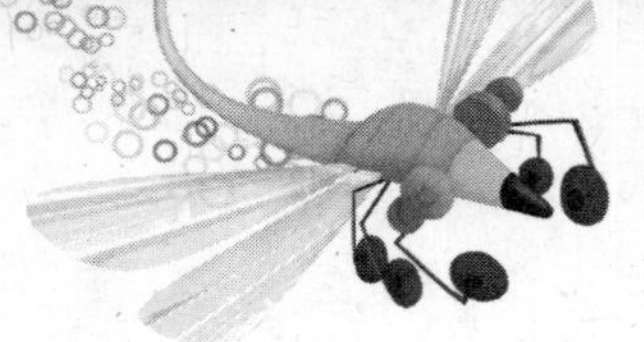

WRITING PROMPT

My Neighborhood

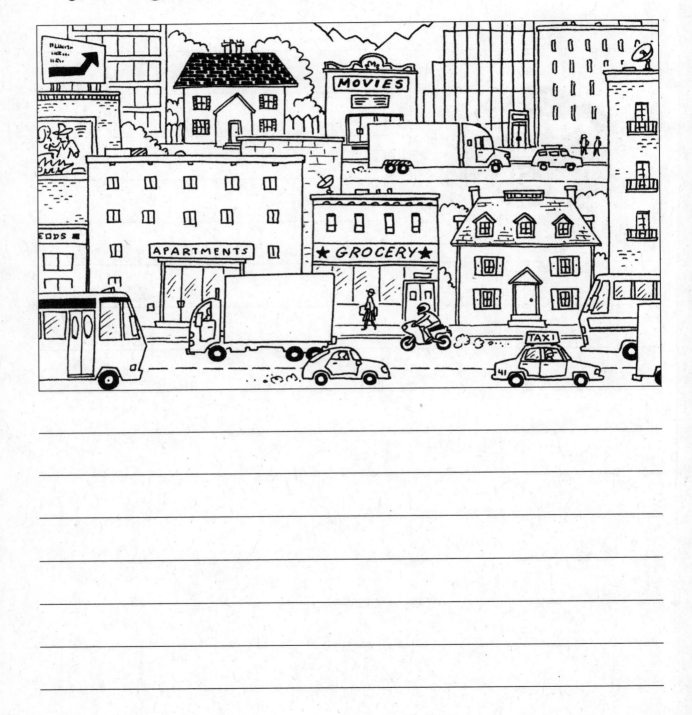

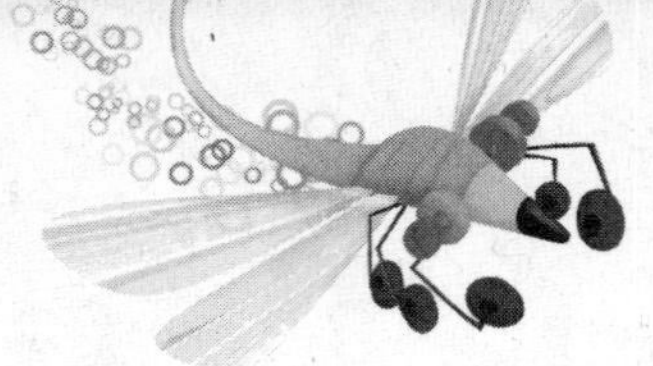

WRITING PROMPT

Shoes tell a lot about a person.

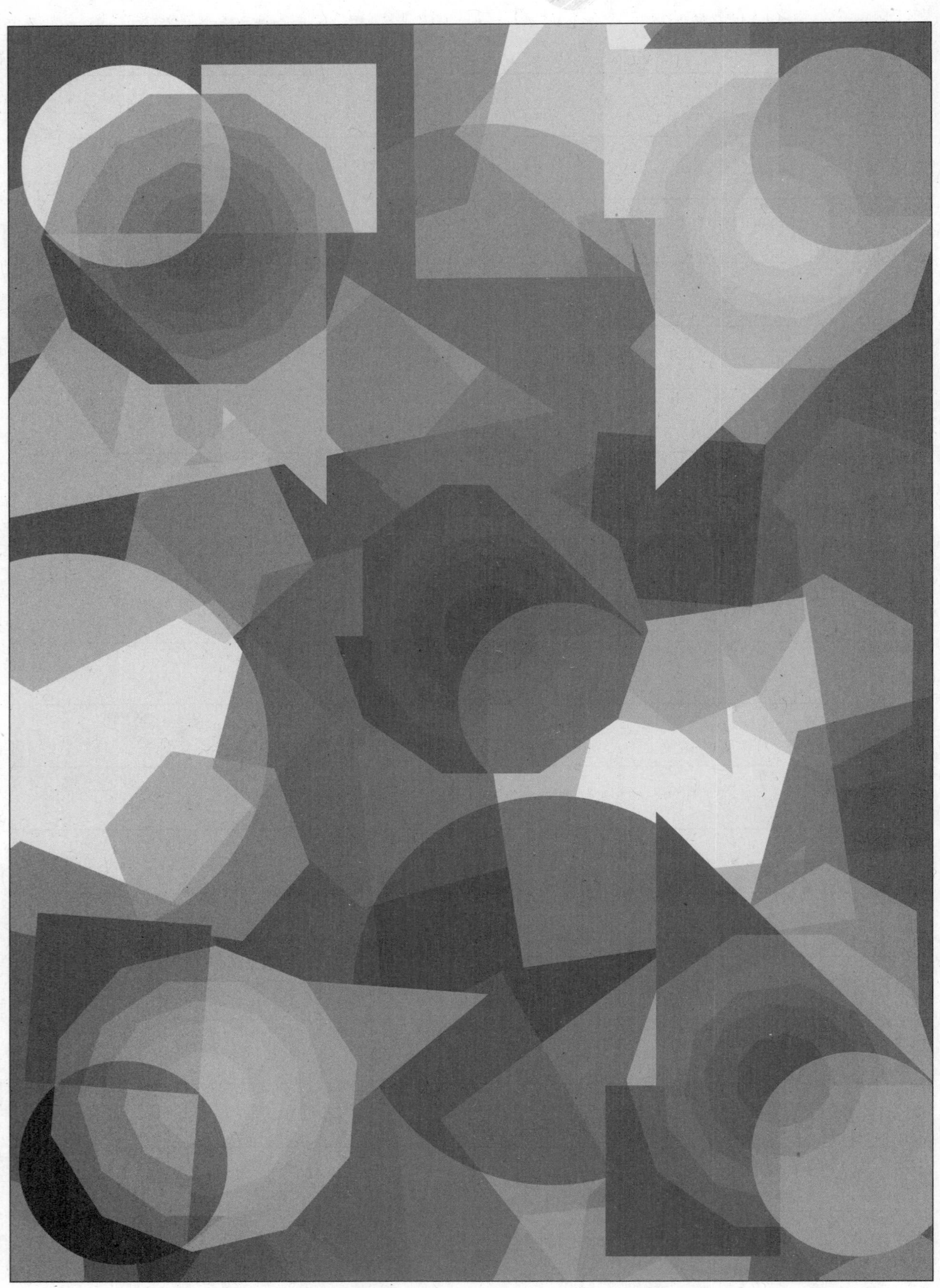

WRITING PROMPT (Write your own.)

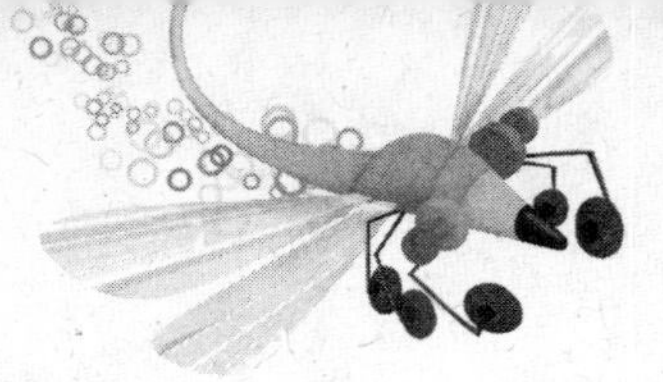

WRITING PROMPT

I finally found those keys.

WRITING PROMPT

Cloud Pictures

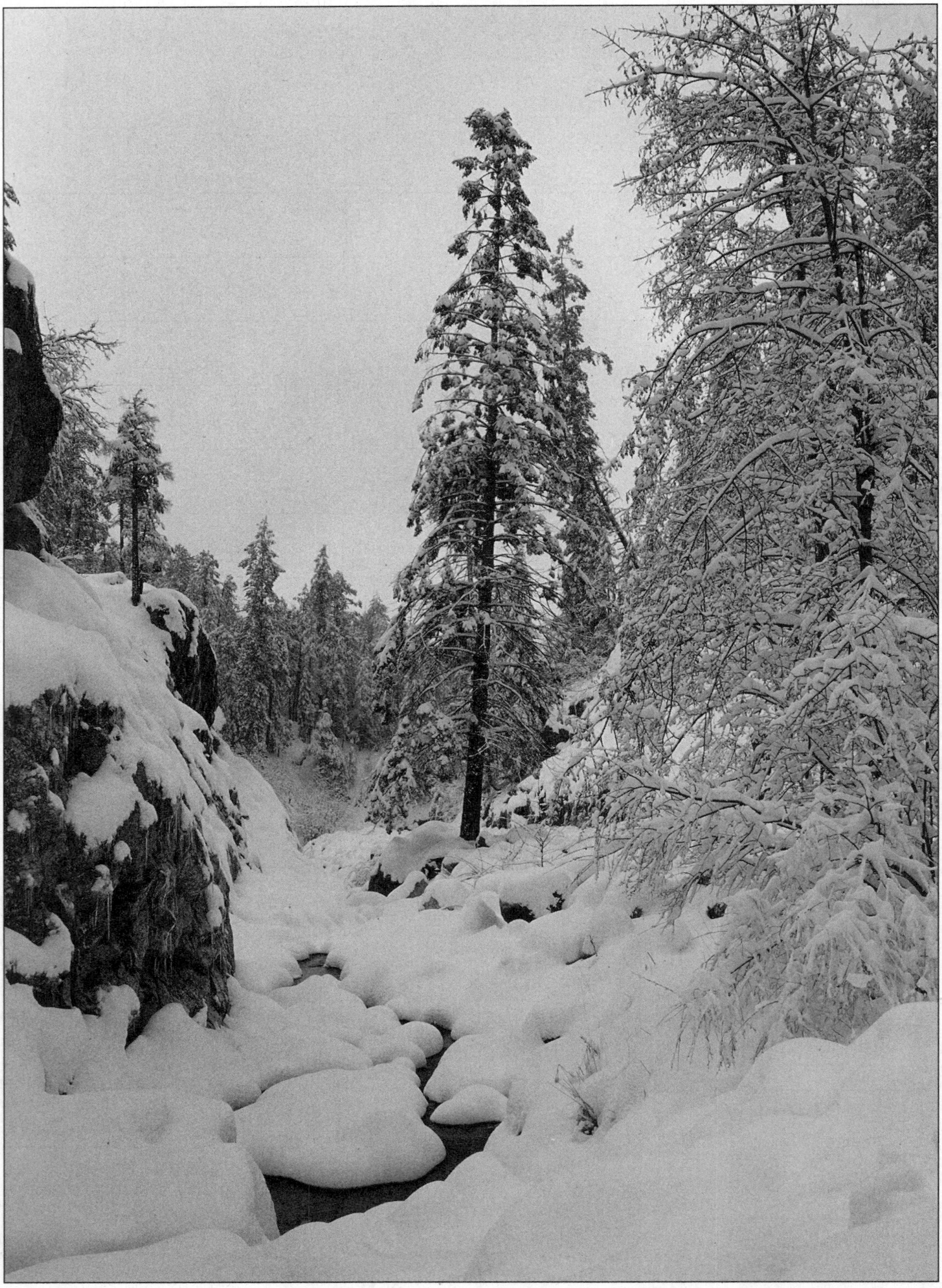

WRITING PROMPT

In winter when it's silent . . .

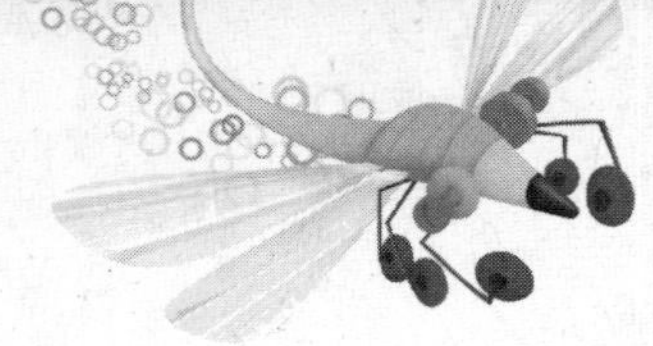

WRITING PROMPT

On the Coast

Writing Topics

Daily Journal Writing

> "I can tap into [my students'] human instinct to write if I help them realize that their lives and memories are worth telling stories about, and if I help them zoom in on topics of fundamental importance to them."
>
> —writing teacher JUNE GOULD

As classroom teachers, we know from firsthand experience that the personal stories young learners love to share can serve as the basis of an effective and lively writing program. Here's how we did it:

Getting Started

At the beginning of the school year, we introduced in-class journal writing to the students. (We encouraged them to write outside of class in journals as well, but the journals in school were part of our writing program.) We knew that the most effective way to get students into writing was simply to let them write often and freely about their own lives, without having to worry about grades or turning their writing in. This helped them develop a feel for "real" writing—writing that originates from their own thoughts and feelings.

That's where the journals come in. Nothing gets students into writing more effectively than a personal journal. (And no other type of writing is so easy to implement.) All your students need are spiral notebooks, pens, time to write, and encouragement to explore whatever is on their minds.

We provided our students with four or five personal writing topics each time they wrote. They could use one of these topics as a starting point, or write about something else entirely. The choice was theirs. (We found that providing writing topics was easier and more productive than just saying "You've got plenty to write about.")

Writing Topics

To start off an exercise, we posted suggested writing topics like these:

- your most memorable kitchen-related experience,
- coping with brothers or sisters,
- being home alone, late at night, or
- what you did over the weekend.

Students would either choose from the list or write on a topic they preferred. See pages 141–144 in this booklet for more suggested topics. We asked our students to write every other day for the first 10 minutes of the class period. (Every Monday, Wednesday, and Friday were writing days.) Of course, we had to adjust our schedule at times, but, for the most part, the students wrote three times a week.

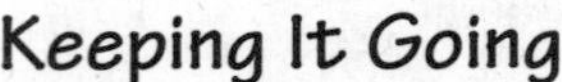

Keeping It Going

After everyone was seated and roll was taken, the journals were passed out, the topics were given, and everyone wrote. We expected students to write for a full 10 minutes, nonstop. They knew that they would earn a quarterly journal grade based on the number of words they produced. This almost made a contest out of the writing sessions. Each time they wrote, they wanted to see if they could increase their production from past journal entries, and they always wanted to write more than their classmates.

> "Over the last fifteen years, a number of teachers around the country and their students have been amazed by what happened when people write ten to fifteen minutes without worrying about grammar, spelling, or punctuation, and concentrate only on telling some kind of truth."
>
> —KEN MACRORIE

Wrapping It Up

On days that we weren't writing, we shared journal entries. First, each student would exchange journals with a classmate. He or she would count the number of words in the latest entry, read it carefully, and then make comments on things he or she liked or questioned. After each pair had shared their comments with one another, we would talk about the entries as a class.

Many writers themselves would be reluctant to share their entries with the entire class. But the readers had no problem volunteering someone else's entry ("You've got to hear Nick's story") and reading it out loud. The students loved these readings and the discussions that followed.

Personal Experience Papers

Periodically, we would interrupt the normal course of journal writing and sharing and make formal writing assignments. That is, we would ask students to review their entries and select one (or part of one) to develop into a more polished, complete, personal experience paper. Usually, those entries that readers enjoyed and wanted to know more about would be the ones the young writers would choose to develop.

We wanted to make sure that their writing went through at least one or two thorough revisions, so we gave our writers plenty of class time to work on their papers. We also required them to turn in all preliminary work with their final drafts. (See "Narrative Writing—Sharing an Experience," pages 75–112, in *Write Source* for guidelines for this type of writing.)

The experience papers were shared with the entire class at the end of the project. This was a fun and informal activity, but one that students came to appreciate as an important part of the entire composing process. It was their day. They were on stage. They were sharing the culmination of all their hard work—a special moment in their own lives.

Writing Topics

Possibilities

- If I could . . .
- If I could have three wishes . . .
- If I could play any instrument . . .
- If I could fly . . .
- If I could climb a mountain . . .
- If I could buy anything . . .
- If I could build a clubhouse . . .
- If I could live anywhere . . .
- If I could visit my hero . . .
- If I could travel back in time . . .

Characterization

- If I were . . .
- If I were incredibly smart . . .
- If I were a superhero . . .
- If I were a teacher . . .
- If I were unable to see colors . . .
- If I were an animal . . .
- If I were 10 feet tall . . .
- If I were as old as my grandparents . . .

Titles

- A Campfire Tale
- My Grandma the Race Car Driver
- A Mixed-Up Day
- The Broken Alarm Clock
- Timmy the Turtle's Adventure
- Cereal with Mustard on Top
- The Longest Tunnel
- When the Tornado Hit
- My Grandpa the Storyteller

School Life

- A project I worked hard on
- My favorite thing to do at recess
- Waiting for the bus
- I like/dislike singing in our school's spring concert.
- What I do when I get home from school
- My most challenging subject
- I wish our class could take a field trip to . . .

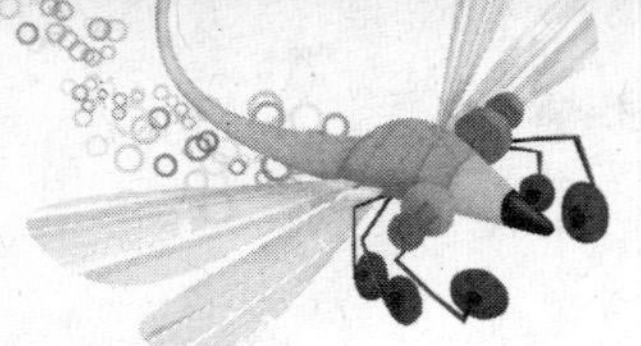

Writing Topics

Me, Myself, and I

- I like/dislike my name because . . .
- When I am 25, this is how my life will be.
- One thing about myself I wish I could change
- The best thing about me
- The best gift anyone ever gave me
- I was really, really looking forward to it, and then . . .
- My most prized possession
- A day of my favorite foods
- I could do this all day long.

Family Life

- Pets in my family
- I wish my family was different.
- This is how I know my parents care about me.
- A typical dinner at my house
- Things I like to do with my parents
- When I visit my grandparents
- My favorite relative

Friends

- A perfect day with my best friend
- Sometimes I wish I could tell my friend . . .
- A time when my friends were mean to me
- The last birthday party I went to

This 'n' That

- I visited the animal shelter and wanted to adopt all the animals!
- If squirrels ruled the world . . .
- I am going to write a book.
- Earthquake!
- I thought I would be grounded for a month.
- A job everyone would like to have

Definitions

- A friend is . . .
- A good vacation is . . .
- A good book is one that . . .
- A playground is . . .
- A father is . . .
- Laughter is . . .
- A computer is . . .

Writing Topics

Nature

- A big fish in a small lake
- Once I saw a . . . in my neighborhood.
- A tree that got hit by lightning
- Should people keep wild animals as pets?
- I know that bats are good to have around, but they give me the creeps!
- One way to be a good citizen of the earth
- I was glad it was raining.
- A sky full of stars

Take Sides

- Year-round school
- Animal rights
- School uniforms/dress codes
- School security
- Video games
- Television/Internet viewing regulations
- Organized sports for elementary grades

Questions

- How are coral reefs being protected?
- How are bridges made?
- What is life like in a submarine?
- What's it like in the kitchen of a zoo?
- How do grocery stores and restaurants get all their fresh food?
- Where do authors get their ideas for the books they write?
- Are car fumes dangerous to the atmosphere?
- What dog makes the best pet?
- How is vegetable oil made from sunflowers, corn, and peanuts?
- How are subways built?
- How are buildings made to resist earthquakes?
- What are highways made of?
- How do window washers get fresh water on the 50th floor?

Writing Topics

Either/Or

- Would I rather play a sport or be a spectator?
- Would I prefer reading the book or seeing the movie?
- Would I rather climb a mountain or go to a mall?
- Would I choose to ride a horse or a snowmobile?
- Would I rather go snorkeling or spelunking?
- Would it be more fun to go down a white-water river or go on a roller coaster?
- Would I rather explore an ocean beach or a history museum?
- Would I rather play the piano or a set of drums?
- Would I rather sing a song or dance to music?
- Would I rather write a letter or play a video game?
- Would I rather take a photo or draw a picture?

Compare/Contrast

- Metric to American measurements
- Hand tools to power tools
- Meat to vegetables
- Freedom to slavery
- Light to darkness
- Cross-country skiing to snowmobiling
- Mountain climbing to scuba diving
- A house to an apartment
- Being strong to being funny
- Leading to following
- Winning to losing

Show-Me Sentences

Producing Writing with Detail

From time immemorial teachers have said to their students, "Your essay lacks details" or "This idea is too general" or "Show, don't tell." We even know of a teacher who had a special stamp made: "Give more examples."

So how should this problem be approached? It's obvious that simply telling students to add more details and examples is not enough. Even showing them how professional writers develop their ideas is not enough (although this does help). Students learn to add substance and depth to their writing through regular practice.

Here's one method that has worked for many students and teachers: the Show-Me sentences. Students begin with a basic topic—"My locker is messy," for example—and create a paragraph or brief essay that *shows* rather than *tells.* The sentence is a springboard for lively writing.

About Your Show-Me Sentences . . .

The following pages contain 45 Show-Me sentences. Each sentence speaks directly to students, so they should have little difficulty creating essays full of personal details. Again, we suggest that you use these sentences every other day for an extended period of time (at least a month).

Note: By design, each page of Show-Me sentences can be made into an overhead transparency.

Implementation

DAY ONE Before you ask students to work on their own, develop a Show-Me sentence as a class. Start by writing a sample sentence on the board. Then have students volunteer specific details that give this basic thought some life. List their ideas on the board. Next, construct a brief paragraph on the board using some of these details. (Make no mention of the original sentence in your paragraph.) Discuss the results. Make sure that your students see how specific details help create a visual image for the reader. Also have your students read and react to examples of "showing writing" from professional texts. (Share the sample of "showing writing" on page 147 with your students.)

DAY TWO Have students work on their first Show-Me sentences in class. Upon completion of their writing, have pairs of students share the results of their work. Then ask for volunteers to share their writing with the entire class. (Make copies of strong writing for future class discussions.)

DAY THREE Ask students to develop a new paragraph. At the beginning of the *next* class period, discuss the results (break into pairs as before). Continue in this fashion for at least a month.

Note: Reserve the first 5 or 10 minutes of each class period for writing or discussing. (Students who don't finish their writing in class should have it ready for the next day.)

Evaluation

Have students reserve a section in their notebooks for their writing or have them compile their work in a folder. At regular intervals, give them some type of performance score for their efforts. At the end of the unit, have them select one or two of their best examples to revise and then submit for a thorough evaluation.

Enrichment

In *Writers in Training,* Rebekah Caplan developed an extensive program to help students produce well-detailed, engaging essays. She made the following suggestions:

- Have your students turn cliches like *It's a small world* or *Accidents will happen* into strong narrative or descriptive paragraphs.
- Have them develop sentences like *Friday nights are better than Saturday nights* into paragraphs that compare and contrast two subjects.
- In addition, have students convert loaded statements like *Noon hours are too short* or *I don't need a bedtime* into opinion pieces.

Note: In a sense, these variations become progressively more challenging. Most student writers, for example, have more difficulty supporting an opinion than they have illustrating the basic ideas behind a cliche.

- You might also use vocabulary words from science, math, social studies, and so forth, in Show-Me sentences or connect these sentences to literary works under study. (Generally speaking, Show-Me sentences can be linked to any unit of study.)

Sample Writing

■ **The twins are different as night and day.** ***(cliche)***

Even though Jack and Zack are identical twins, they don't seem to have much in common. Jack wears glasses, and Zack does not. Jack dyed a green streak in his short, spiky hair, while Zack has a buzz cut. Jack prefers sweats, but Zack likes jeans and button-down shirts. Their personalities are different, too. Jack is funny and loud. Zack is serious and quiet. They have different friends at school, too.

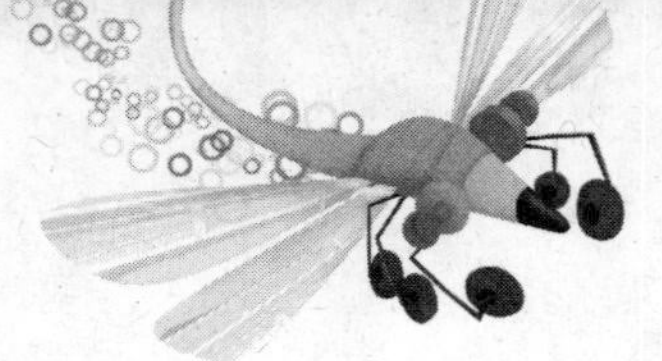

SHOW-ME SENTENCES

- The toy was damaged.

- The birthday party was fun.

- It was raining hard.

- My brother can make large bubbles.

- The sunset was pretty.

SHOW-ME SENTENCES

- I've never been so embarrassed.
- This puppy is cute.
- I enjoyed myself at the fair.
- The bird flew away.
- I read a great book.

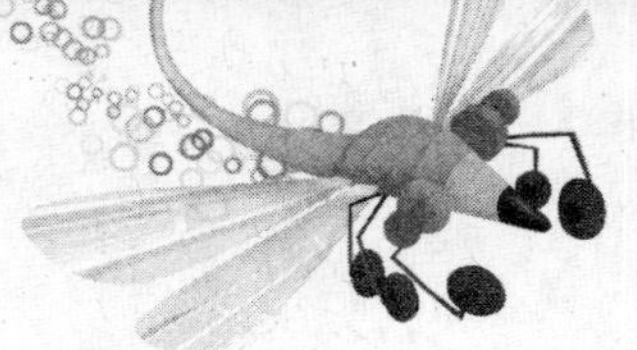

SHOW-ME SENTENCES

- That movie is so funny.

- The people next door are noisy.

- She looked angry.

- The old house seemed mysterious.

- Our game ended in victory.

SHOW-ME SENTENCES

- The telephone rang.

- An aardvark is an awkward animal.

- I like the color ______________________.

- This old blanket is so comfortable.

- Those burgers tasted awful.

SHOW-ME SENTENCES

- Skateboarding is awesome.

- The bad weather made them late.

- The shrubs are overgrown.

- She has a small stuffed animal.

- My uncle is one in a million.

SHOW-ME SENTENCES

- We had a short vacation.
- The siren caught his attention.
- The shore was littered.
- They had an accident.
- Lemons are sour.

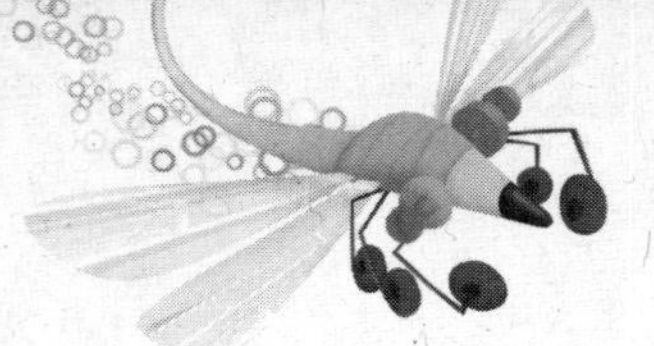

SHOW-ME SENTENCES

■ We always work in a careful manner.

■ She has beautiful hair.

■ The night was black as coal.

■ They dug a deep hole.

■ He was unusually flexible.

SHOW-ME SENTENCES

- We decorated the room for the party.
- This empty box could be useful.
- The boat floated on the lake.
- __________ is my prized possession.
- Thanksgiving is a pleasant holiday.

SHOW-ME SENTENCES

- He doesn't like that food.

- She left in a hurry.

- My cat is sweet.

- He was grouchy.

- The elevator moved very slowly.